Mac OS X
Pocket Guide

D0760217

SECOND EDITION

Mac OS X
Pocket Guide

Chuck Toporek

O'REILLY®

Beijing · Cambridge · Farnham · Köln · Paris · Sebastopol · Taipei · Tokyo

Mac OS X Pocket Guide, Second Edition

by Chuck Toporek

Published by O'Reilly & Associates, Inc., 1005 Gravenstein Highway North,
Sebastopol, CA 95472.

O'Reilly & Associates books may be purchased for educational,
business, or sales promotional use. Online editions are also available
for most titles (*safari.oreilly.com*). For more information, contact our
corporate/institutional sales department: (800) 998-9938 or
corporate@oreilly.com.

Editor:	Chuck Toporek
Production Editor:	Linley Dolby
Cover Designer:	Emma Colby
Interior Designer:	David Futato

Printing History:

May 2002:	First Edition.
November 2002:	Second Edition.

0-596-00458-3
[C]   [6/03]

Contents

Part III. System Tools

Part IV. Mac OS X Unix Basics

Part V. Task and Setting Index

Mac OS X
Pocket Guide

Introduction

As with any operating system, new changes and improvements are welcomed with somewhat skeptical arms. As news about Jaguar, the latest version of Mac OS X (10.2), started to leak out of Apple's Worldwide Developer Conference (WWDC), Apple's groundbreaking OS took on a fervor of epic proportions. The Mac suddenly became *the* machine to have for users and developers alike.

This new edition of the *Mac OS X Pocket Guide* is intended to be a quick reference to Mac OS X Jaguar, and has something for everyone:

- If you're an experienced Mac user, this book may be the only one you'll need. For Mac users coming to Mac OS X from an earlier version of the Mac OS, some of the material in this book can serve as a refresher, reminding you how to do certain things you've always been able to do on the Mac. In addition, you'll learn more about the Unix side of Mac OS X and how to use its command-line interface, the Terminal application.

- If you're a Unix, Linux, or FreeBSD user who is switching to the Mac, you'll get a quick summary of how to use Mac OS X's interface and how to use its Terminal application for issuing Unix commands. If you're looking for something more hardcore, I recommend that you pick up a copy of *Mac OS X for Unix Geeks*, which covers such things as Directory Services, use of Mac OS X's GCC compiler, installing packages with Fink, and running X Windows on top of Mac OS X.

- If you're a Windows user, you'll get a quick tour of the operating system, along with a guide to help you relate some Windows-specific terms to your Mac. While the Terminal and Unix commands will be all new to you, they're not too far off from the DOS prompt commands you've used in the past.

With over 250 tips and tricks, this *Pocket Guide* is a handy reference for configuring and working with your Mac OS X system.

Conventions Used in This Book

The following typographical conventions are used in this book:

Italic

Used to indicate new terms, URLs, filenames, file extensions, directories, Unix commands and options, and program names. For example, a path in the filesystem will appear as */Applications/Utilities*.

Constant width

Used to show the contents of files or the output from commands.

Constant width bold

Used in examples and tables to show commands or other text that should be typed literally by the user.

Constant width italic

Used in examples and tables to show text that should be replaced with user-supplied values.

Variable lists

The variable lists throughout this book present answers to "How do I…" questions (e.g., "How do I change the color depth of my display?").

Menus/navigation

Menus and their options are referred to in the text as File → Open, Edit → Copy, etc. Arrows will also be used to signify a navigation path when using window options; e.g., System Preferences → Screen Effects → Activation means you would launch System Preferences, click on the icon for the Screen Effects preferences panel, and select the Activation pane within that panel.

Pathnames

Pathnames are used to show the location of a file or application in the filesystem. Directories (or *folders* for Mac and Windows users) are separated by forward slashes. For example, if you see something like, "…launch the Terminal application (*/Applications/Utilities*)" in the text, that means the Terminal application can be found in the *Utilities* subfolder of the *Applications* folder.

↵

A carriage return (↵) at the end of a line of code is used to denote an unnatural line break; that is, you should not enter these as two lines of code, but as one continuous line. Multiple lines are used in these cases due to printing constraints.

%, #

The percent sign (%) is used in some examples to show the user prompt for the *tcsh* shell; the hash mark (#) is the prompt for the *root* user.

NOTE

Indicates a tip, suggestion, or general note.

WARNING

Indicates a warning or caution.

Menu symbols

When looking at the menus for any application, you will see some symbols associated with keyboard shortcuts for a particular command. For example, to open a document in Microsoft Word, you could go to the File menu and select Open (File → Open), or you could issue the keyboard shortcut, ⌘-O.

Figure 1 shows the symbols used in the various menus to denote a keyboard shortcut.

Control   Shift   Option   Command

Figure 1. Keyboard accelerators for issuing commands

Rarely will you see the Control symbol used as a menu command option; it's more often used in association with mouse clicks to emulate a right click on a two-button mouse, or for working with the *tcsh* shell.

PART I

Mac OS X Survival Guide

This first part is intended to show those who are new to Mac OS X how to acclimate quickly to their new environment. For Windows and Unix users who are Switching to Mac OS X, most everything will be new, while users of older versions of Mac OS, such as Mac OS 8 or 9, will have to adjust the most to relearn the Mac.

This part of the book covers:

- Changes to Mac OS X from Mac OS 9
- Tips for "Switchers" coming to Mac OS X from Windows and Unix systems such as Linux or one of the BSDs (FreeBSD, NetBSD, or OpenBSD)

Changes to Mac OS X from Mac OS 9

There are many noticeable changes in the user interface from earlier versions of the Mac OS to Mac OS X, while others may not be so apparent. Two of the biggest changes from Mac OS 9 to Mac OS X can be found in the Apple menu and the Control Panels.

The Apple Menu

The Apple menu, displayed as an apple symbol () in the menu bar, is completely different; you can no longer store aliases for files, folders, or applications there. Here's what you'll find in Mac OS X's Apple menu:

About This Mac

This option pops open a window that supplies you with information about your Mac. Aside from telling you that you're running Mac OS X on your computer, the window shows you which version of Mac OS X is installed, how much memory you have, and the speed and type of processor in your computer. Clicking on the More Info button launches the Apple System Profiler (*/Applications/ Utilities*), which gives you a greater level of detail about your computer.

TIP

Clicking on the version number in the About This Mac window will reveal the build number of Mac OS X; clicking it again will show the hardware serial number for your computer. These small details are important to have when contacting Apple Customer Service and when reporting a probable bug.

In earlier versions of the Mac OS, the About box would change depending on which application was active. For information about the application, you now have to use the Application menu (located to the right of the Apple menu) and select the About option.

Get Mac OS X Software

Selecting this option will take you to Apple's Mac OS X software page (*http://www.apple.com/downloads/macosx/*) in your default web browser.

System Preferences

Launches the System Preferences application, which replaces most of the Control Panels from earlier versions of the Mac OS. See "System Preferences" later in this book for more details.

Dock

This menu offers a quick way to change settings for the Dock (described later).

Location

This is similar to the Location Manager Control Panel from earlier versions of the Mac OS; it allows you to change locations quickly for connecting to a network and/or the Internet.

Recent Items

This menu option combines the Recent Applications and Recent Documents options from Mac OS 9's Apple menu into one convenient menu. A Clear Menu option allows you to reset the recent items from the menu.

Force Quit

Thanks to Mac OS X's protected memory, you don't have to restart the entire system if an application crashes or freezes. Instead, you can come here (or use Option-⌘-Esc) to open a window that lists the applications running on your system. To Force Quit an application, simply click on the application name, then click on Force Quit.

Unlike applications, you cannot force quit the Finder by Control-clicking on its icon in the Dock. Instead, you need to restart it from here. When you select the Finder, the Force Quit button changes to Relaunch; click that button to restart the Finder.

Sleep

Selecting this option immediately puts your Mac into sleep mode. This is different from the settings you dictate in System Preferences → Energy Saver for auto-sleep functionality. To "wake" your computer from sleep mode, simply press any key.

If you close the lid (or display) on your iBook or Power-Book while it is running, the computer goes into sleep mode. Opening your laptop wakes up your system automatically.

Restart

This restarts your Mac. If any applications are running, they will be automatically shut down, and you will be prompted to save changes for any files that were open.

Shutdown

This shuts down your Mac. You can also shut down your Mac by pressing the Power-On button, which will open a dialog box with the options for restarting, shutting down, or putting your Mac to sleep.

Log Out

This option logs you out of your system, taking you back to a login screen. The keyboard shortcut to log out is Shift-⌘-Q.

NOTE

Sleep, Restart, Shutdown, and Log Out have moved from Mac OS 9's Special menu into Mac OS X's Apple menu. If you're looking for a menu option for Empty Trash, you will need to be in the Finder (Finder → Empty Trash, or Shift-⌘-Delete).

Think System Preferences, Not Control Panels

One of the most notable changes in Mac OS X is that the Control Panels (⍟ → Control Panels) aren't in the Apple menu. The Control Panels of old are now replaced by System Preferences. Table 1 lists the Control Panels from Mac OS 9 and shows you their equivalents in Mac OS X.

Table 1. Mac OS 9's Control Panels and their disposition in Mac OS X

Mac OS 9 Control Panel	Equivalent in Mac OS X
Appearance	System Preferences → Desktop System Preferences → General
Apple Menu Options	System Preferences → General
AppleTalk	System Preferences → Network → AppleTalk
ColorSync	System Preferences → ColorSync
Control Strip	Gone; replaced by Dock
Date & Time	System Preferences → Date & Time
DialAssist[a]	System Preferences → Network → Show → Internal Modem
Energy Saver	System Preferences → Energy Saver
Extensions Manager	Gone. With Mac OS X, you no longer need to manage your extensions. To view the extensions on your system, launch the Apple System Profiler (*/Applications/Utilities*), and click on the Extensions tab.
File Exchange	Gone
File Sharing	System Preferences → Sharing
File Synchronization	Gone
General Controls	System Preferences → General
Infrared	System Preferences → Network → Show → infrared-port
Internet	System Preferences → Internet
Keyboard	System Preferences → Keyboard System Preferences → International → Input Menu
Keychain Access	Applications → Utilities → Keychain Access
Launcher	Gone; replaced by Dock
Location Manager	System Preferences → Network → Location (This only applies to network settings, unlike Location Manager.) → Location
Memory	Gone
Modem	System Preferences → Network → Show → Internal Modem
Monitors	System Preferences → Displays

Mac OS 9 Control Panel	Equivalent in Mac OS X
Mouse	System Preferences → Mouse
Multiple Users	System Preferences → Accounts
Numbers	System Preferences → International → Numbers
Password Security	Available on new machines via open firmware
QuickTime Settings	System Preferences → QuickTime
Remote Access	Applications → Internet Connect
Software Update	System Preferences → Software Update
Sound	System Preferences → Sound
Speech	System Preferences → Speech
Startup Disk	System Preferences → Startup Disk
TCP/IP	System Preferences → Network
Text	System Preferences → International → Language
Trackpad	System Preferences → Mouse

a Not available under Classic.

See "System Preferences," later in this book, for additional information about each control.

Other Missing Items

Some other things you'll find missing from Mac OS X include:

Apple CD Audio Player
> This has been replaced by iTunes.

The Chooser
> To configure a printer in Mac OS X, you need to use the Print Center (*/Applications/Utilities*). To connect to a server or another computer on your network, you need to use Go → Connect to Server (⌘-K). The Chooser still exists for printing and networking from the Classic environment (described later).

Put Away (⌘-Y)

> This command had two functions: to eject a disk (floppy or CD), or to move an item out of the Trash back to its place of origin. Instead, ⌘-E can be used to eject a CD or unmount a networked drive.

TIP

On newer iBooks and PowerBooks, pressing the F12 key will eject a CD or DVD.

Graphing Calculator

> Gone; no replacement.

Note Pad and SimpleText

> These have been replaced by the much more versatile TextEdit application.

NOTE

If you installed the Developer Tools, SimpleText can be found in */Developer/Applications/Extras*, but it isn't available otherwise.

Scrapbook

> The Scrapbook has gone to the scrap heap.

SimpleSound

> This has been replaced by the Sound panel, which can be accessed from System Preferences → Sound → Alerts.

Tips for Switchers

If you're one of the many people who have finally decided to make the "Switch" to Mac OS X from Windows or another Unix operating system (such as FreeBSD, Solaris, or Linux), this section is intended to be a quick reference guide to aid in your transition to the Mac. I've tried to point out some key differences between your old platform and Mac OS X to help you acclimate yourself with your Mac.

General Tips for Switchers

The following tips apply (in general terms) to Switchers from both Windows and other Unix-based systems, as well as users who've made the transition from Mac OS 9 to Mac OS X:

- The Mac user interface has only one menu bar—at the top of the screen—instead of one on each window. The menu bar's contents change depending on which application is currently active. The name of the application that's currently active appears in bold text next to the Apple menu.

- At first, you will sorely miss your two- or three-button mouse. You can emulate right-button functions by holding down the Control key when clicking. Mac OS X also supports multibutton mice, mapping the Control key to the right mouse button.

- If you have a scrollwheel mouse, Mac OS X should detect it automatically and provide options for how the scrollwheel performs via the System Preferences → Mouse preferences panel.

- To find what Mac OS X applications you have on your system, click on the Applications icon in the Finder's toolbar.

- To find out which Mac OS 9 applications you have on your system, click on Finder → Computer → Macintosh HD → Applications (Mac OS 9).

- Printer setup and queue control is handled by the Print Center application (*/Applications/Utilities*). You may want to drag it onto the Dock or place its icon in the Finder toolbar for easy access.

- Each user has his own desktop, which is stored in */Users/ username/Desktop*. By default, many documents (such as

---

files downloaded from the Web or saved attachments) are stored in */Users/username/Documents*. Files stored in the Desktop folder will appear on the desktop when you log in.

- Looking for an update to some piece of software you're running on your system? Check out Version Tracker (*http://www.versiontracker.com*).

If you're a Mac OS 9 user and you are on the fence about switching or upgrading to Mac OS X, now's the time to get off that fence and upgrade. Mac OS X is a more stable operating system than Mac OS 9, and you can still run your Mac OS 9 applications on top of Mac OS X in the Classic environment.

Tips for Windows Switchers

If you're coming to the Mac from a Windows system, these tips are for you:

- The Apple menu, located at the far left of the menu bar, is roughly analogous to the Windows Start menu (although it doesn't list common utilities).

- The basic GUI control program, akin to the Windows Explorer or the Window Manager in Windows, is called the Finder. Clicking on its icon in the Dock (the blue smiley-face icon) brings up a Finder window, not the desktop, as you might expect.

- System Preferences is analogous to the Windows Control Panel. The System Preferences application can be launched by clicking on its icon in the Dock (the one that looks like a light switch with a gray apple next to it).

- The Dock is analogous to the Windows Task Bar. It is initially populated with some frequently accessed applications, such as the Finder, System Preferences, and Sherlock. You can drag any program icon onto the Dock to create a shortcut to it accessible at all times.

- The Command key (⌘) provides many of the functions that you are used to having associated with the Control key. For example, use ⌘-C to copy, not Control-C; ⌘-S to save, not Control-S; etc.

- If you're accustomed to using Alt-Tab to switch between active applications, you should use ⌘-Tab to do the same thing on the Mac. (Even though the Option key does say "alt" on it, the Option key doesn't do the same things that the Alt key does on a Windows system.)

- You can use StuffIt Expander (/Applications/Utilities) to unzip files by double-clicking on the Zip archive.

- You can zip up files from the command line in the Terminal application (/Applications/Utilities). See the "Task and Setting Index" for examples on how to Zip and unzip files from the command line.

- If you really want Windows, you can install Virtual PC, which allows you to run Windows applications on top of Mac OS X.

NOTE

Windows users will benefit most from David Pogue's new book, *Switching to the Mac*, co-published by Pogue Press and O'Reilly & Associates.

Tips for Unix Switchers

If you're coming to Mac OS X from another Unix OS, these tips are for you:

- The Unix command line (the *tcsh* shell) is available via the Terminal application (/Applications/Utilities). If you plan to work frequently from the command line, you should add the Terminal application's icon to the Dock by dragging its icon there.

- The available user shells include *bash*, *csh*, *sh*, *tcsh* (the default), and *zsh*; *bash* is the default for shell scripts instead of *zsh* as in earlier versions of Mac OS X.

- While Mac OS X is Unix-based, it doesn't come with the X Window System. You can download and install a rootless version of X, but first you should download and install Fink (*http://fink.sourceforge.net*), which you can use to download and automatically install X Windows and other BSD Unix applications.

- While the Terminal application gives you a command-line interface, it is slightly different from an *xterm*. For example, the Terminal doesn't have a *.xinitrc* file from which to control how Terminal windows appear. Instead, use Terminal → Show Info (⌘-I) to configure your Terminal's appearance.

- For Unix users and administrators, you'll quickly find out that some of the standard admin commands are missing or that useful options aren't there. For example, the commands for managing users and groups don't exist; for that, you need to use the System Preferences panels, and/or NetInfo Manager (*/Applications/Utilities*).

- To find out which Unix applications and utilities are available, you can poke around in */usr/bin*, */usr/local/bin*, */usr/sbin*, */usr/share*, and */usr/libexec*.

TIP

To quickly list all the binary executables on your system, use Control-X Tab or Control-X Control-D to list all the binaries in the Terminal.

- By default, the *root* user (or *superuser*) isn't activated. If you are the only user on your system, you will have administrator privileges by default, which allows you to use the *sudo* command. See "The root User Account" later in this book for details on how to activate the *root* user.

NOTE

For most tasks, the *sudo* command should suffice. Enable the *root* user account only if you must, taking into consideration the possible security risks that go along with a *root*-enabled system.

- Looking for virtual desktops? Give Space (by Riley Lynch) a try (*http://space.sourceforge.net*).

- Speaking of Sourceforge (*http://www.sourceforge.net*), you'll find lots of freeware applications and utilities for Mac OS X here, as you have in the past for Linux and freeBSD.

- If you're a Unix developer or system administrator, we suggest you pick up a copy of *Mac OS X for Unix Geeks* (O'Reilly), which covers things such as the Terminal, Directory Services and NetInfo, compiling code with GCC, installing packages with Fink, and running the X Windows System on top of Mac OS X.

PART II

Mac OS X Basics

This part of the book will introduce you to the key features of the Mac OS X interface. Here we'll cover:

- Window Controls
- The Finder
- Keyboard shortcuts
- The Dock
- Mac OS X and the Classic Environment
- Users and Logging in Window Controls

Window Controls

Windows in Mac OS X have an entirely different set of controls than those from earlier versions of the Mac OS. These window features are highlighted in Figure 2.

The controls are defined as follows:

1. Close window button (red)
2. Minimize window button (yellow)
3. Zoom, or maximize, window button (green)
4. Proxy icon
5. Filename
6. Toolbar button (not available on all windows)
7. Scrollbars and scroll arrows
8. Resize window control

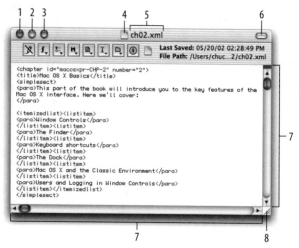

Figure 2. Standard window controls in Mac OS X

The top part of the window is known as the *titlebar*. The titlebar is home to the three colored window control buttons for closing (red), minimizing (yellow), and zooming (green) the window. Mousing over the buttons will change their state to be either an X, a minus sign (–), or a plus sign (+), respectively. These are visual cues to you as to the function the button performs.

With some applications, you'll notice that the red close window button has a dark-colored dot in its center. This means that the document you're working on has unsaved changes; if you save the document (File → Save, or ⌘-S), the dot will go away.

Window Tips

The following are some tips for working with windows:

Open a new window?
    File → Open (⌘-O).

Close a window?
    File → Close (⌘-W).

Close all open windows for an application?
    Option-click on the close window button.

TIP

If there are changes that need to be saved in any of the windows being closed, you will be prompted to save the changes. Either hit Return to save the changes, or enter ⌘-D to invoke the Don't Save button.

Minimize a window?
    Window → Minimize Window (⌘-M).

    Double-click on the window's titlebar.

Minimize all open windows for a single application?
    Option-⌘-M.

NOTE

With some applications, Option-⌘-M may function differently. For example, issuing Option-⌘-M in Microsoft Word (Office v.X) will open the Paragraph format window (Format → Paragraph). To be safe, you should save changes to the file before trying to minimize all the application's windows with Option-⌘-M.

Quickly create an alias of an open file, or move it, depending on the app (e.g., Word)?
    Click and drag the file's proxy icon to a new location (i.e., the Desktop, Dock, Finder, etc.). The file must first be saved and named before an alias can be created.

Find out where the file exists in the filesystem?

Command-click on the proxy icon. This will pop open a context menu, showing you where the file exists. Selecting another item (such as a hard drive or a folder) from the proxy icon's context menu will open a Finder window taking you to that location.

Hide the windows for other active applications?

Option-⌘-click on the Dock icon for the application you're using, and the open windows for all other active applications will instantly hide. To bring another application's windows to the front, click on that application's Dock icon, or to unhide all the other windows, select Show All from the application menu (Finder → Show All).

The Finder

In earlier versions of the Mac OS, the Finder was located in the application menu at the far-right edge of the menu bar. The Finder was the application responsible for displaying the contents of a drive or folder; when double-clicked, a window would open, displaying either an Icon or List View of the contents. Mac OS X's Finder really isn't that different from Mac OS 9's Finder. It still displays the contents of drives and folders; however, the Finder is much more powerful, particularly in Jaguar.

The Finder serves as a graphical file manager, which offers three ways (or *Views*) to look at the files, folders, applications, and other filesystems mounted on your system. The Finder also sports a toolbar that allows you quick access to frequently used files and directories, along with a built-in Search field. More on the Finder toolbar and how to search for files later; for now, let's look at the three Views available to the Finder: Icon, List, and the new Column View.

TIP

You can quickly change the Finder's viewpoint by using ⌘-1 for Icon View, ⌘-2 for List View, or ⌘-3 for Column View.

Icon View

This shows the contents of a directory as either a file, folder, or application icon, as shown in Figure 3. Double-clicking on an icon will do one of three things: launch an application, open a file, or display the contents of a double-clicked folder in the Finder window.

Figure 3. The Finder in Icon View

Table 2 presents a list of keyboard shortcuts that can be used within the Finder's Icon View.

Table 2. Icon View's keyboard shortcuts

Key command	Description
Up, Down, Left, and Right Arrow keys	Move through the icons in the View based on the key pressed.
Shift-Arrow key	When one icon is selected and the Shift-Arrow (Up, Down, Left, or Right) keys are pressed, the icon in that direction will be selected as well.

List View

A directory's contents are displayed in a list, as shown in Figure 4. To display the contents of a folder, you can click on the disclosure triangle (the black triangle to the left of the folder), as illustrated in the figure.

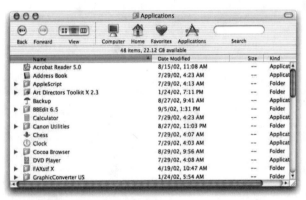

Figure 4. The Finder in List View

Another way to navigate through the icons and folders in the Finder's List View is by using the keyboard, as noted in Table 3.

Table 3. List View's keyboard shortcuts

Key command	Description
Down Arrow	Move down through the list of items.
Up Arrow	Move up through the list of items.
Right Arrow	Open a folder's disclosure triangle to reveal its contents.
Left Arrow	Close a folder's disclosure triangle to hide its contents.
Option-Right Arrow	Open a folder and any subfolders.
Option-Left Arrow	Close a folder and any subfolders.

To open all the folders in the View, select all the View's contents (⌘-A) and use Option-Right Arrow (likewise, use Option-Left Arrow to close them again). To open all the folders in the View, including subfolders, add the Shift key (Shift-Option-Right Arrow to open, Shift-Option-Left Arrow to close).

Column View

For NeXT users, the Column View will look familiar. Column View, shown in Figure 5, displays a directory's contents in column form. This is similar to List View, except that when you click on an item, a new pane opens to the right and either exposes the contents of a folder or displays some information about a file, including its name, type, and file size.

Table 4 lists the keyboard shortcuts that can be used within the Finder's Column View.

Table 4. Column View's keyboard shortcuts

Key command	Description
Up, Down, Left, Right Arrow keys	Move through the columns in the View based on the key pressed

The Finder's application menu has options for changing the Finder's preferences (Finder → Preferences), and for emptying the trash (Finder → Empty Trash, or Shift-⌘-Delete).

Figure 5. The Finder in Column View

The Finder Toolbar

Near the top of the Finder window is a toolbar (shown in Figure 6), which offers a quick way to access files and directories on your system and also to switch between the View modes mentioned earlier.

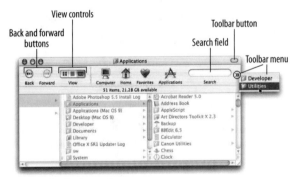

Figure 6. The Finder toolbar

You can add a file, folder, or application to the Finder toolbar by dragging and dropping its icon to the toolbar. Application icons that get added to the toolbar will launch with a single click, just as they do in the Dock.

Located at the upper-right corner of the Finder window is a clear, elliptical button that can be used to hide the Finder's toolbar, as shown in Figure 7.

Figure 7. The Finder window with a hidden toolbar

If you are in Icon or List View with the toolbar hidden, the Finder window performs just like Mac OS 9's Finder windows. Double-clicking on a folder icon will open a new window for that folder, displaying its contents. Column View will function normally.

Searching from the Finder

As seen in Figure 6, the Finder's toolbar sports a Search field. This is a new feature, added for Mac OS X 10.2 (Jaguar), replacing Sherlock's old system search functionality.

To search for a file on your system, simply type a word in the Search field and hit Return. The search begins from the location selected in the Finder window and traverses through the filesystem from that point. For example, if you are in your home directory (e.g., ~/chuck) the search looks inside all your user directories.

Search results are displayed in a split Finder window, as shown in Figure 8. Note that the titlebar for the Search Results window also displays the item you searched for and the directory from which the search was conducted.

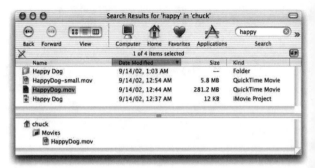

Figure 8. The Finder's search results window

Clicking on one of the items in the search results in the upper pane displays its path in the lower pane. Double-clicking a folder opens that location in the Finder window; double-clicking an application icon launches the application; and double-clicking a file opens the file in the appropriate application (and launches that application, too, if it isn't already active).

You can also do a more advanced search by clicking on the "Search" text label below the search field. This opens up the Find window (shown in Figure 9), which is also the same Find window you'll see if you select File → Find (⌘-F).

Clicking on the Search button will open a window, revealing the search results.

Finder Tips

The following are some tips for working with the Finder:

Hide the Finder toolbar?
    View → Hide Toolbar (⌘-B).

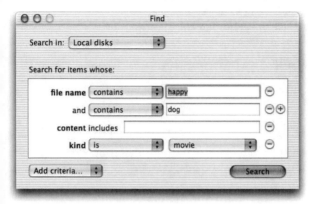

Figure 9. The Finder's Find window

Click on the transparent button in the upper-right corner of the titlebar.

Customize the Finder toolbar?

Finder → View → Customize Toolbar.

Shift-click the toolbar button.

Control-click within the toolbar and select Customize Toolbar from the context menu.

Shift-clicking on the toolbar button again closes the Customize Toolbar window and returns you to the previous Finder View.

Only show the icons or text labels of items in the toolbar?

View → Customize Toolbar → Show; select Icons Only or Text Only from the pull-down menu.

Speed up Finder searches?

Open the Finder's preferences panel (Finder → Preferences). Click on the Select button at the bottom of the window; this pops open a window that lets you select the languages to use when searching a files' contents. The fewer languages you select here, the faster your search.

Locate a specific folder in the Finder?
    Go → Go to Folder (or Shift-⌘-G).

Keyboard Shortcuts

On the Mac (as with Windows and Linux desktops), you
have two ways of invoking commands in the GUI: by using
the menus or by issuing shortcuts for the commands on the
keyboard. Not every menu item has a keyboard accelerator,
but for the ones that do—the more common functions—
using the keyboard shortcuts can save you a lot of time.

Basic Keyboard Shortcuts

Table 5 lists the common key commands found in Mac OS X.
While most of these commands function the same across all
applications, the functions of some, such as ⌘-B and ⌘-I, can
vary between programs, and others may only work when the
Finder is active. For example, ⌘-B in Microsoft Word turns
on boldface type or makes a selection bold, while in Project
Builder, ⌘-B builds your application. Likewise, ⌘-I in Word
italicizes a word or selection, while hitting ⌘-I after selecting
a file, folder, or application on the Desktop or in the Finder
opens the Show Info window for the selected item.

Table 5. Common keyboard shortcuts

Task	Key command
Open the Force Quit window	Option-⌘-Escape
Cycle through active applications in the Dock	⌘-Tab
Cancel operation	⌘-.
Open Mac Help	⌘-?
Go back in the Finder view to the previous item	⌘-[
Go to a folder in the Finder	Shift-⌘-G
Select all	⌘-A
Hide/reveal the Finder's toolbar	⌘-B

Table 5. Common keyboard shortcuts (continued)

Task	Key command
Copy	⌘-C
Duplicate; creates a duplicate copy of a selected item. This command adds the word "copy" to the filename before the file extension. For example, if you were to select the file *file.txt* and hit ⌘-D, a new file named *file copy.txt* (with a space in the filename) would be created in the same directory as *file.txt*.	⌘-D
Turn Dock hiding on/off	Option-⌘-D
Move item to Trash	⌘-Delete
Empty Trash	Shift-⌘-Delete
Eject the selected disk image, CD, etc.	⌘-E
Find	⌘-F
Hide application	⌘-H
Get Info	⌘-I
Show View options in the Finder.	⌘-J
Connect to Server	⌘-K
Make alias	⌘-L
Minimize window	⌘-M
Minimize all open windows for an application	Option-⌘-M
Open a new Finder window. (This is a change from earlier versions of the Mac OS where ⌘-N was used to create new folders.)	⌘-N
Create new folder	Shift-⌘-N
Open file or folder; can also be used to launch applications.	⌘-O
Print file	⌘-P
Quit application	⌘-Q
Show original	⌘-R
Add an item to the Favorites menu	⌘-T
Paste	⌘-V
Close window	⌘-W
Close all open windows for an application	Option-⌘-W
Cut	⌘-X

Table 5. Common keyboard shortcuts (continued)

Task	Key command
Undo	⌘-Z
Redo (not available in all applications)	Shift-⌘-Z
Go to Applications View in the Finder	Shift-⌘-A
Go to Computer View in the Finder	Shift-⌘-C
Go to Favorites View in the Finder	Shift-⌘-F
Go to Home View in the Finder	Shift-⌘-H
Go to iDisk View in the Finder (requires a .Mac account)	Shift-⌘-I
Take a screenshot of the entire display	Shift-⌘-3
Make and capture a rectangular selection of the display	Shift-⌘-4

Startup and Shutdown Keys

For most users, starting and shutting down your Mac is fairly routine: press the Power-on button to start, and go to ⍟ → Shut Down to turn off the machine at night. But there are times when you need to do more, for whatever reason. Table 6 lists some of the additional keys you can use when starting, restarting, logging out, and shutting down your system.

NOTE

Some of the keyboard shortcuts listed in Table 6 will work only on newer hardware. If you are using an older Mac, these keyboard shortcuts may not work.

Table 6. Keyboard shortcuts for starting, restarting, logging out, and shutting down

Key command	Description
C	Holding down the C key at startup will boot from a CD (useful when installing or upgrading the system software).
T	Holding down the T key at startup will boot from a FireWire drive, if it has a bootable System folder.

Table 6. Keyboard shortcuts for starting, restarting, logging out, and shutting down (continued)

Key command	Description
X	Holding down the X key at startup will force the machine to boot into Mac OS X, even if Mac OS 9 is specified as the default startup disk.
⌘-S	Boots into single-user mode.
⌘-V	Boots into verbose mode, displaying all the startup messages onscreen. (Linux users will be familiar with this.)
Shift	Holding down the Shift key at startup invokes *Safe Boot* mode, turning off any unnecessary kernel extensions (*kexts*), and ignoring anything you've set in the Login Items preferences panel.
Option	Holding down the Option key at startup will take you to the Startup Manager, which allows you to select which OS to boot into.
Mouse button	Holding down the mouse button at startup will eject any disk (CD, DVD, or other removable media) that may still be in the drive.
Shift-Option-⌘-Q Option + 🍎 → Log Out	Logs you off without prompting you first.
Option-Power-on Option + 🍎 → Shut Down	Shuts down your system without prompting you first.
Option + 🍎 → Restart	Restarts your machine without prompting you first.
Control-⌘-Power-on button	Forces an automatic reboot of your system; this should be used only as a last resort as it could mess up your system.[a]

[a] Mostly, you'll just wait forever at the gray apple startup screen while an *fsck* happens in the background.

The Dock

One way to think about the Dock is as part Finder, part Apple menu, and part Launcher from earlier versions of the Mac OS. The Dock, shown in Figure 10, holds application aliases, making it easy for you to launch a program quickly with a single mouse click. To launch an application in the

Dock, simply click on its icon. While the application is starting, its icon will "bounce" in the Dock; afterward, a black triangle will appear below the icon to indicate that the application is active.

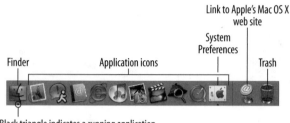

Figure 10. The Dock

By default, the Dock includes icons for the Finder, Mail, iChat, Address Book, Internet Explorer, iTunes, iPhoto, iMovie, Sherlock, QuickTime, System Preferences, and the Trash. To the left of the Trash icon is a quick link icon to Apple's Mac OS X web site; clicking this icon will launch your default web browser and take you to Apple's web site.

NOTE

The Finder icon is permanently fixed to the left of the Dock (or on top if you've moved your Dock to the left or right of the screen). Likewise, the Trash is located at the far-right of the Dock (or at the bottom if your Dock is on the left or right). No matter how hard you try to grab and move them around, you can't. Also, you can't place an icon to the left of the Finder or to the right of the Trash.

To add an application icon to the Dock, simply drag its icon from the Finder to any location in the Dock and let go. To remove an application, click on the icon and drag it away from the Dock; the icon will disappear in a puff of smoke.

Using and Configuring the Dock

Here are some helpful hints and tips for using and configuring your Dock:

Quickly resize the Dock without launching its System Preferences panel?

> Place the mouse over the divider bar in the Dock; the pointer changes from an arrow to a horizontal bar with arrows pointing up and down. Click on the divider bar and move the mouse up or down to make the Dock larger or smaller, respectively.

Change the Dock's preferences?

> → Dock → Dock Preferences.

> System Preferences → Dock.

> Control-click on the Dock's divider bar and select Dock Preferences from the context menu.

Add a program to the Dock?

> Drag and drop an application's icon in the Dock from a Finder window.

> After launching an application that isn't normally in the Dock, Control-click on that application's icon, and select "Keep in Dock" from the pop-up menu.

Remove a program from the Dock?

> Drag the application icon from the Dock and drop it anywhere.

Change the Dock's location from the bottom of the screen to the left or right side?

> System Preferences → Dock → Position on screen.

> → Dock → Position on (Left, Bottom, or Right).

> Control-click on the Dock's divider and select Position on screen → (Left, Bottom, or Right).

Control the magnification of icons in the Dock?

> System Preferences → Dock → Magnification.

→ Dock → Turn Magnification (On/Off).

Control-click the Dock's divider and select Turn Magnification (On/Off).

Make it so the Dock hides when I'm not using it?

Option-⌘-D.

System Preferences → Dock → Automatically hide and show the Dock.

 → Dock → Turn Hiding (On/Off).

Control-click the Dock's divider and select Turn Hiding (On/Off).

Stop application icons from bouncing when a program is launched?

System Preferences → Dock → Animate opening applications. Instead of the application's icon bouncing, the disclosure triangle next to the icon will pulse until the program is fully launched.

Dock Tricks

The following key-mouse commands can be used when clicking on an icon in the Dock:

Command-click

If you ⌘-click an application icon in the Dock (or just click and hold down the mouse button), the Finder will open, taking you to that application's folder.

Shift-⌘-click

Opens a Finder window to the application's location in the filesystem. This is similar to Control-clicking a Dock icon and selecting Show In Finder from its context menu.

Control-click

If you Control-click a running application in the Dock (or click and hold down the mouse button), a pop-up menu will open, listing the windows that the application has open, as well as options to show the application in the Finder and to Quit the application.

If you press the Option key while Control-clicking an icon in the Dock, the Quit option will toggle to Force Quit. This will not work for Classic applications (i.e., it only works for native Mac OS X applications).

Option-click

Option-clicking has the same effect as Control-clicking, with one exception: Quit has been replaced by Force Quit in the pop-up menu.

Option-⌘-click

Hides the windows of all other open applications and switches (if necessary) to the clicked application; similar to selecting Hide Others from an the application menu.

Command-Tab

The ⌘-Tab function allows you to cycle through and switch between running applications quickly. As you press ⌘-Tab, the icons for running applications will highlight; when you release the ⌘ key, you will be taken to that application.

Shift-⌘-Tab

Shift-⌘-Tab has the reverse effect of ⌘-Tab, in that it moves backward through running applications in the Dock.

NOTE

If you choose Empty Trash from the Dock by clicking on the icon and holding down the mouse button, the Trash icon's pop-up menu will empty locked files as well.

Mac OS X and the Classic Environment

To help bridge the application gap between Mac OS 9 and Mac OS X, Apple has built a *virtual machine* that enables you to run older Mac software under Mac OS X in what's known as *Classic*. Classic (or the "Classic environment") looks and feels just like Mac OS 9. The only exception is that the applications that are run in Classic don't benefit from the features of Mac OS X, such as protected memory and advanced printing capability. Additionally, some Control Panels (→ Control Panels), such as Control Strip, Memory, and Remote Access, are disabled.* Basically, when you're running Classic, you are running a slightly watered-down version of Mac OS 9 *on top of* Mac OS X with only a minor performance hit.

Until all Mac applications are compliant with Mac OS X, you will also need to install a version of Mac OS 9 (9.2.2, to be exact). During the installation process, you can install both Mac OS 9 and Mac OS X on the same partition (or hard drive), or you can use Disk Utility (Installer → Open Disk Utility) to create a separate partition for each. Basically, you're creating a *dual-boot system*, which means you can boot your Mac into either OS. However, if you don't plan to run Classic applications, you won't need to install Mac OS 9.

If your computer came with Mac OS X preinstalled, Mac OS 9 has been preinstalled as well. It's worth noting that Apple places both Mac OS X and Mac OS 9 on the same partition of your hard drive. If you want the OSes on separate partitions, you will need to partition your hard drive and reinstall the system. In most cases, the biggest benefit of installing Mac OS 9 and Mac OS X on separate partitions is being able to choose a startup volume at boot up by holding down the Option key.

---

* However, if you boot into Mac OS 9 instead of Mac OS X, you will be using a full version of the OS. See later for details on how to choose your Startup Disk.

Otherwise, you can choose which OS to boot using the Startup Disk Control Panel (Mac OS 9) or System Preferences → Startup Disk (Mac OS X). At the time of this writing, Apple will reportedly make it impossible for you to boot into Mac OS 9 on newer hardware that releases in January 2003.

NOTE

If you use the Process Viewer or the *top* command, described later, look for a process named *TruBlueEnvironment*. This is the Classic process—and all the applications running under Classic—in action.

To launch a Classic application, locate the application using the Finder (Finder → Macintosh HD → Applications (Mac OS 9)), and double-click on the application icon. The Classic environment will start if it isn't already running.

NOTE

If you frequently use a particular Classic application, you can also add it to the Dock by dragging its icon to any location in the Dock. However, Control-clicking a Classic application's icon will not reveal a Dock menu; this support is only provided to native Mac applications (Carbon and Cocoa apps).

While it's easy to use a Classic application on files saved on your Mac OS X partition, you will have a hard time accessing files saved on non-AFP networked drives. For example, if you're running Office 2001 and you want to open a Word document (*filename.doc*) on the partition named *Maui*, you won't find that drive in Word 2001's Open dialog. Fortunately, you can use the Terminal application to launch Word 2001 *and* open the file in one fell swoop. To do this, launch the Terminal application (*/Applications/Utilities*), and issue the following command on the command line:

```
open /Volumes/Maui/filename.doc
```

This command instructs your computer to open *filename.doc* (found on */Volumes/Maui*) using Microsoft Word. For more information about how to use the Terminal application, see "Configuring and Using the Terminal" later in this book.

Users and Logging In

When you first install Mac OS X (or when you first boot your new hardware), you have to create at least one user account. Mac OS 9 first introduced the option of setting up a multiuser Mac system, but you weren't required to set up individual user accounts as with Mac OS X.

Tips for Users

Here are some helpful hints to assist you in managing your user account:

Configuring my login?
> System Preferences → Accounts → Login Options.

Change my login password?
> System Preferences → My Account; click on the Change button next to My Password.
>
> System Preferences → Accounts → *username* → Edit User.
>
> Use the *passwd* command in the Terminal.

NOTE

When choosing a password, you should avoid using dictionary words (i.e., common, everyday words found in the dictionary) or something that could be easily guessed. To improve your security, choose an alphanumeric password. Remember, passwords are case-sensitive, so you can mix upper- and lowercase letters in your password as well.

Add another user to the system?

System Preferences → Accounts → New User (requires administrator privileges).

NOTE

Unix administrators might be tempted to use the *useradd*, *userdel*, and *usermod* commands to add, remove, and modify a user, respectively, from the Terminal. The only problem is, *you can't*—those commands don't exist on Mac OS X.

Remove a user from the system?

System Preferences → Accounts → *username* → Delete User (requires administrator privileges). After a user has been deleted, that user's directories (and everything within) is packaged up in a disk image (as *username.dmg*) and placed in the */Users/Deleted Users* folder. This disk image can be deleted only by someone with administrator privileges.

NOTE

When you're logged in, you can't remove yourself from the system. If you want to remove your user account from the system, you have to log out and log back in as another user.

Give a user administrator privileges?

System Preferences → Accounts → *username* → Edit User → Allow user to administer this computer (requires administrator privileges).

Restrict which applications a user can use?

System Preferences → Accounts → *username* → Capabilities. Click on the checkbox next to "Use only these applications," and then use the lower-half of the window to pick and choose the applications to which the user can have access. This only works for users who *do not* have administrator privileges.

Keep a user from changing her password?

System Preferences → Accounts → *username* → Capabilities; uncheck the box next to Change password.

Turn off automatic login?

System Preferences → Accounts → *username*; uncheck the box next to "Log in automatically as *username*."

Allow a user to log in to my Mac from a Windows system?

System Preferences → Sharing → Services; check the box next to Windows File Sharing.

Set a password hint?

The easy way to do this is by going to System Preferences → Accounts. Double-click on your account name and a sheet will slide out of the titlebar. Select any text that's in the Password Hint field, type in a new hint, and click OK to accept the change.

If you go back to the My Account or the Accounts panel, you'll see that the login hint hasn't changed. However, if you quit and relaunch the System Preferences, the change will take effect.

Now for the (sort of) hard way. You can also use Net-Info Manager (*/Applications/Utilities*) to change your password hint. You need to have administrator privileges to perform these steps:

1. Launch NetInfo Manager.

2. Click on the lock at the lower-left corner of the window and enter the admin user's password.

3. In the columns at the top half of the window, select users → *username* (e.g., users → chuck).

4. In the lower-half of the window, click on the hint line in the Property column, then double-click in the Value(s) column.

5. Type in a login hint and hit Return to accept the value.

6. Click on the lock in the lower-left corner of the window to prevent any further changes from being made. When you click on the lock, an alert window will appear; click on the "Update this copy" button to accept the changed login hint.

7. Quit NetInfo Manager.

Find out which users have admin privileges?

System Preferences → Accounts. Users with administrator privileges will have Admin listed next to their names in the Type column.

Launch NetInfo Manager (*/Applications/Utilities*). In the Directory Browser pane, select / → groups → admin. In the lower half of the window, look at the Property value next to users; you'll see something like (root, *username*) in the Value(s) column. (Requires administrator privileges.)

Add a new group?

Launch NetInfo Manager (*/Applications/Utilities*). In the Directory Browser pane, select / → groups. From the menu bar, go to Directory → New Subdirectory (⌘-N). (Requires administrator privileges.)

In the Directory pane below, select the *new_directory* name by double-clicking on it, type in a new group name (e.g., *editorial*), and then click again on *new_directory* in the Directory Browser pane. A warning message will appear, asking you if you want to save the changes (click Save). Another message window will appear, asking you to confirm the modification; click on the "Update this copy" button, and the new group name will be applied in the Directory Browser pane.

NOTE

As with the user-related Unix commands, Unix users will notice that the various group commands (*groupadd*, *groupdel*, *groupmod*, *gpasswd*, *grpconv*, and *grpunconv*) are missing from Mac OS X. You will need to use NetInfo Manager (*/Applications/Utilities*) to manage groups.

User Subdirectories

Once created, each user is provided with a series of subdirectories in his *Home* directory (*/Users/username*). These directories, listed here, can be used for storing anything the user desires, although some have specific purposes.

Desktop

    This directory contains the items found on your Desktop, including any files, folders, or application aliases you've placed there.

Documents

    While it isn't mandatory, the *Documents* directory can be used as a repository for any files or folders you create.

Library

    This directory is similar to the */System/Preferences* directory found in earlier versions of the Mac OS; it contains resources used by applications, but not the applications themselves.

Movies

    This is a place where you can store movies you create with iMovie or hold QuickTime movies you create or download from the Internet.

Music

> This directory can be used to store music and sound files, including *.aiff*, *.mp3*, etc. This is also where the iTunes Library is located.

Pictures

> This directory can be used as a place to store photos and other images. iPhoto also uses the Pictures directory to house its iPhoto Library directory, which contains the photo albums you create.

Public

> If you enable file or web sharing (System Preferences → Sharing), this is where you can place items you wish to share with other users. Users who access your *Public* directory can see and copy items from this directory.

Shared

> If your system has more than one user on it, a Shared directory will be created. Because users are only allowed to add or modify files within their own home directories, this is a place where you can place items to be shared with the other users.

Sites

> If you enable Web Sharing (System Preferences → Sharing → File & Web), this is the directory that will house the web site for your user account.

The root User Account

On any Unix system, the *root* user has the authority to issue any command, giving that user extreme power. Because of the risks associated with that power (such as the ability to permanently delete the entire filesystem), the *root* user account has been disabled by default on Mac OS X. However, there are two ways you can enable the *root* user account: by using NetInfo Manager or from the command line. In both cases, you must already have administrator privileges on the system.

Follow these steps to enable the *root* user account from NetInfo Manager:

1. Launch NetInfo Manager (*/Applications/Utilities*).

2. To make changes to the NetInfo settings, click on the padlock in the lower-left corner of the NetInfo window. You will be asked for the administrator's name and password; enter those, and click OK.

3. In the menu bar, select Security → Enable Root User.

4. You will be asked to enter a password for the *root* user. In earlier versions of Mac OS X, the *root* password had to be eight characters or less; however, in Jaguar, the *root* password must only be more than five characters in length. Click OK, and then enter the password again to confirm the password for the *root* user account. Click on the Verify button to confirm the password and enable the *root* account.

5. If you have no further changes to make in NetInfo Manager, click on the padlock at the lower-left of the window to prevent further changes from being made, and quit the application (⌘-Q).

To enable the *root* user account using the Terminal, enter the following command:

```
[macchuck:~] chuck% sudo passwd root
Password: *******
Changing password for root.
New password: ********
Retype new password: ********
[macchuck:~] chuck%
```

The first time you're asked for a password, enter your own. Once you're verified by the system to have administrator privileges, you will be asked to enter and confirm a new password for the *root* user account.

NOTE

The asterisks shown in this example won't appear on-screen when you enter the passwords; actually, nothing will happen onscreen. If you make a mistake while entering the password, you can always hit the Backspace or Delete key to go back over what you typed; then just re-enter the password.

Once the *root* account has been assigned a password, you can use it to log in with the username *root*.

If you find that you need to access a directory or issue a command that requires *root* (or *superuser*) privileges, you can temporarily log in as the *root* user by issuing the *su* command:

```
[macchuck:~] chuck% su
Password: ********
[MacChuck:/Users/chuck] chuck#
```

Notice how the prompt has changed from chuck% to chuck#. The # prompt is an indicator that you are running as *root*. As *root*, you should be careful about what you type.

After you've finished your business as *root*, type *exit*, and hit Return to log out as the *root* user and return to your normal user prompt.

NOTE

The *root* user's home directory can be found in */private/var/root*.

Get Info and Setting File Permissions

Get Info gives you access to all sorts of information about the files, directories, and applications on your system. To view the information for an item, click on its icon in the Finder, and either go to File → Get Info or use its keyboard shortcut, ⌘-I. The Get Info window has six different panes, which offer different kinds of information about the file. To reveal the content of one of these items, click on its disclosure triangle to expand the pane. The panes of the Get Info window include the following:

General

> This tells you the basics about the file, including its kind, size, where it's located in the filesystem, and when it was created and last modified.

Name & Extension

> This displays a text box with the name of the file or directory.

Content index

> This pane is only available when you use Get Info on a folder or directory (not with individual files); it tells you whether the contents of a folder have been indexed. Indexing stores information about the files contained within that directory in an information database used by the Find command when searching for files on your system. To index a folder, click on the Index Now button; this may take some time, depending on how many files or folders are contained within the folder.

Open with Application

> This option is only available if you select a file (i.e., not a folder or an application). Here you can specify which application will open this file or all similar files.

Preview

> Depending on the file type, you can view the contents of the file here (this also works for playing sounds and QuickTime movies).

Ownership & Privileges
> This displays the name of the owner and the name of the group to which the file belongs. It also allows you to set access privileges to that file for the Owner, Group, and Others on the system.

Comments
> This field can contain some basic information about the file, folder, or application.

The Get Info window for applications has the General Information, Name & Extension, and Ownership & Privileges options mentioned previously (although the Ownership & Privileges options are disabled by default), as well as one or both of the following options:

Languages
> Shows the languages supported by that application.

Plug-ins
> If applicable, this lists the available plug-ins for the application. iPhoto's Info window has a Plug-ins section.

Noticeably missing from a Mac OS X application's Get Info window is the Memory option. Because memory for applications is assigned dynamically by virtual memory, you no longer have to specify how much memory an application requires. However, if you use Get Info on a Mac OS 9 application, the Memory option will be there.

PART III

System Tools

This part introduces you to the various tools that accompany Mac OS X. The sections in this part are intended to provide an overview of the following:

- System Preferences
- Applications and Utilities
- Developer Tools

The "Task and Setting Index" provides additional information about how to use and apply the System Preferences for configuring your system, as well as specific uses for some of Mac OS X's standard Applications and Utilities.

System Preferences

As mentioned earlier, Mac OS X's System Preferences perform many of the same functions as Mac OS 9's Control Panels. To launch the System Preferences application, simply click on the light-switch icon in the Dock, and the window shown in Figure 11 will appear.

As you'll notice, the System Preferences are broken down into four categories: Personal, Hardware, Internet & Network, and System. There is also a customizable toolbar at the top of the window, similar to the toolbar in the Finder window. If you find yourself using a particular System Preference often, drag its icon to the toolbar. Likewise, if there is one you use rarely (such as the Displays panel), drag the icon away, and the item will be removed from the toolbar.

Toolbar —

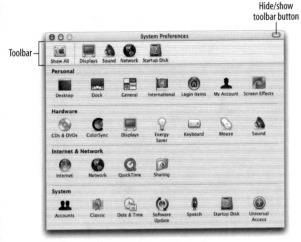

Figure 11. The System Preferences window

Unlike the Finder's toolbar, you cannot customize the System Preferences toolbar. (You can customize the Finder's toolbar by Control-clicking on the toolbar itself and selecting Customize Toolbar from the context menu.) Thankfully, not all hope is lost, though. You can add and remove icons from the System Preferences toolbar by dragging an icon onto or off the toolbar. When you drag an icon off the toolbar, it will disappear in a puff of smoke, similar to what happens when you remove an icon from the Dock. You can also change the size of the icon and the text labels for the icons by Command-clicking on the toolbar button as follows:

- The first time you Command-click reduces the size of toolbar icons and the text labels.

- The second time you Command-click removes the text labels and displays the icons at the normal size.

- The third time you Command-click reduces the size of the toolbar icons without the text labels.

- The fourth time you Command-click removes the panel icons and replaces them with large text labels.

- The fifth time you Command-click reduces the size of the text labels without the panel icons.

- The sixth time you Command-click returns the icons and text labels for the panels in the toolbar to their normal, original size.

NOTE

This also works in applications such as Mail and the Omi applications (such as OmniWeb, OmniGraffle, and OmniOutliner). If you add the Shift key to any of these ⌘-click combinations (i.e., Shift-⌘-click), you'll go backward through the cycle to the previous setting.

You can move the icons in the toolbar around by click-dragging them to a different position. The only icon you can't remove from the toolbar is the Show All icon, which is permanently fixed to the far left of the toolbar. Additionally, you can't place anything to the left of the divider bar in the toolbar.

When you click on one of the icons, the window changes to reflect that particular panel's settings, but the toolbar remains in place. To hide the toolbar, click on the transparent button in the upper-right corner of the window. To go back to the main view, click the Show All button (View → Show All In Categories, or ⌘-L). You can also select View → Show All Alphabetically; this menu option changes the view of the System Preferences window to that shown in Figure 12.

When you've completed altering the settings of your computer, quit the System Preferences (System Preferences → Quit, or ⌘-Q).

The next four sections provide an overview of the controls found in the System Preferences. For additional information on how to use the System Preferences panels to configure your system, see the "Task and Setting Index" later in the book.

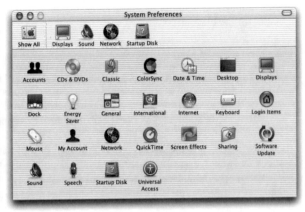

Figure 12. The System Preferences, listed alphabetically

NOTE

Some of the System Preferences panels require administrator privileges. If you attempt to change a setting and are asked for a password, try using the password you used to log in to the computer. If that doesn't work, contact your system administrator for assistance.

Personal

These items control the general look and feel of the Aqua interface:

Desktop

This lets you set the pattern, image, or color of your desktop. If you click on the checkbox next to Change picture at the bottom of the window, the desktop picture will change automatically based on the timing you select in the pull-down menu.

Dock

This is one of the ways you can configure your Dock (another is by going to → Dock → Dock Preferences).

See "Using and Configuring the Dock," earlier in the book, for details on the Dock.

General

This panel specifies the colors used for buttons and menu items when selected, location of scrollbar arrows (top and bottom, or together, known as "Smart Scrolling" in Mac OS 9), and how a click in the scrollbar will be interpreted (scroll down one page or scroll to that location in the document). Here, you can specify the number of recent items to be remembered and listed in the → Recent Items menu for Applications and Documents, as well as determine which font smoothing style and size is best for your type of display.

International

This is used to set the languages supported by your system. The language you specify during the installation process will be the default. Also found here are controls used to format the date, time, numbers, and currency, as well as the keyboard layout to be used for a country and its language.

If you select more than one language in the tabbed Input Menu pane, a menulet will appear in the menu bar, showing the flags for the countries whose languages will be supported on your system.

Login Items

This panel lets you specify which items will launch or open automatically after you log in to your system. These "items" can include applications, files, folders, and remote filesystems. For Mac OS 9 users, the Login Items panel is similar to placing an alias in the *Startup Items* folder.

My Account

This panel includes options for changing your password, specifying a login picture (from either one of 30 default images or from another on your system), and an option for editing your card in the Address Book. You can further configure your account via the Accounts panel, described later.

Screen Effects

This panel lets you select one of Mac OS X's default screensaver modules. Here, you can set the amount of time your system must be inactive before the screensaver kicks in, require a password to turn off the screensaver, and specify Hot Corners for enabling/disabling the screensaver.

If you have a .Mac account, you can also choose from the .Mac Screen Effects, or subscribe to another .Mac member's public slide show. To do this, click on the Configure button and enter the members' name (for example, *chuckdude*).

Hardware

These panels are used to control the settings for the devices connected to your computer.

Bluetooth

This panel allows you to configure the settings for using Bluetooth to exchange files with other users and to synchronize data between your computer and other devices, such as cellular phones and PDAs. This item only appears if you have a Bluetooth USB dongle (such as the one Apple promotes from D-Link) inserted on your system.

CDs & DVDs

The items in the CDs & DVDs panel all share the same basic interface: a pull-down menu that lets you choose what the Mac does when it mounts various kinds of disks. You can choose to have it simply open the new media volume as a Finder window, launch an appropriate application (such as iTunes for music CDs and Disk Copy for blank discs), run a script, or prompt you for some other action to take.

ColorSync

This panel is used to control and ensure the quality of the colors you see on your monitor.

Displays

This panel lets you set your monitor's resolution and its color-depth (256, thousands, or millions of colors). There is also an option to include a monitor menulet in the menu bar, as well as a slider control to set your monitor's brightness. If you have more than one monitor connected to your system, clicking on the Detect Displays button will allow you to specify settings for that display.

Energy Saver

This panel is used to set the auto-sleep settings for your computer. Here, you can specify the amount of time your system must be idle before putting your monitor, hard drive, or the entire system to sleep.

PowerBook and iBook users will also see two pull-down menus at the top of this panel. The first, Optimize Energy Settings, lets you select from one of four preset options, or to specify custom settings. The second pull-down menu, Settings for, gives you options for controlling the Energy Saver settings for when you're plugged in (Power Adapter), or when you're operating on battery (Battery Power).

Ink

This item appears only if you have a graphics tablet (such as a Wacom tablet) connected to your system. Ink controls how handwritten text is handled by the InkPad. The Gestures tab includes pen-strokes for invoking commands such as Undo, Cut, Copy, Paste, inserting a space or carriage return (Vertical Space), and more.

Keyboard

This panel controls the repeat rate when you depress a key and hold it down. You can specify the speed of the repeat (from slow to fast) and the delay between the time the key is first depressed until the repeat option kicks in (from long to short). If you select the Off option for Delay Until Repeat, the repeat feature will be disabled entirely.

If you click on the Full Keyboard Access tab and opt to "Turn on full keyboard access," you can use the Control key with either Function keys, Letter keys, or Custom keys instead of using the mouse. These key combinations and their functions are listed in Table 7.

Table 7. Keyboard Access key combinations

Function keys	Letter keys	Description
Control-F1	Control-F1	Enable/disable keyboard access
Control-F2	m	Control the menu bar
Control-F3	d	Control the Dock
Control-F4	w	Activate the window or the next window behind it
Control-F5	t	Control an application's toolbar
Control-F6	u	Control an application's utility window (or palette)
Control-F7	Control-F7	Used for windows and dialogs to highlight either text input fields and lists, or for any window control
Esc	Esc	Return control to the mouse, disabling the Control-Fx key combination
Spacebar	Spacebar	Perform the function of a mouse click

NOTE

If you are using an iBook or PowerBook, you need to use Control plus the *fn* key along with the Function or Letter key for keyboard access; for example, Control-fn-F2 to access menus. The *fn* key is at the bottom-left corner of your keyboard, to the left of the Control key (and below the Shift key).

Mouse

This panel lets you specify the mouse's Tracking Speed, as well as the delay between double-clicks. If you are using an iBook or PowerBook, the Mouse preferences panel will have an added section for setting the controls for your trackpad.

Sound

This panel offers two panes, one for configuring Alert sounds and another for sound Output (e.g., speakers). The Alerts pane has an option for including a volume control slider in the menu bar.

Internet & Network

These panels are used to control your Mac's settings for connecting to other computers:

Internet

This panel has four tabbed panes. The first two, .Mac and iDisk, allow you to configure the settings for your .Mac account (formerly known as iTools), and supply you with information about your iDisk (requires a .Mac account).

The other two tabbed panes, Email and Web, allow you to enter the settings for your primary email account, specify your default email client and web browser, and choose where files you download from the Internet will be saved.

WARNING

If you have a primary email account (such as the one you use at work or that is provided by your ISP), clicking on the checkbox next to "Use .Mac Email account" will replace the settings for your primary mail account. You will be warned about this by the system; just make sure this is what you really want to do before clicking on the Replace button or hitting Return to dismiss the alert.

Most email clients provide support for multiple mail accounts, including Mac OS X's Mail application. If you have a .Mac email account that's secondary to your primary email account, you should configure the .Mac account in your email client, rather than here in the Internet preferences panel.

Network

This panel is used to configure your settings for dial-up, Ethernet, and AirPort networking, including enabling/disabling AppleTalk. For details on how to configure these settings, see the "Task and Setting Index" later in this book.

QuickTime

This panel lets you configure QuickTime's settings for playing back movies and music. If you've purchased a license for QuickTime Pro, click on the Registration button to enter the registration number.

Sharing

This panel has changed a lot since Mac OS X 10.1.*x*. The Sharing panel is used to set the name of your computer, and your Rendezvous name. The lower portion of the Sharing panel has three tabbed panes:

Services

This pane allows you to turn on file, web, and printer sharing, control FTP access to your machine, and allow users of other computers to log in to your machine remotely via the Secure Shell (SSH).

Firewall

By default, the firewall is turned off. Use this panel to restrict people from the outside world from gaining access to your machine through its various ports and services. The services you turn on in the Services pane controls the enabled services in the Firewalls pane. For example, if you turn on Personal File Sharing in the Services pane, the checkbox next to Personal Fire Sharing will be checked in the Firewall pane.

Internet

This pane allows you to share your Internet connection with other computers, either via AirPort or built-in Ethernet.

System

The items in the System panel allow you to configure a variety of settings for your computer:

Accounts

> As the name implies, this panel is used to add and remove users and to make changes to their identities and passwords.
>
> If you have administrator privileges, you can also specify the Capabilities of a non-administrator's account, for doing such things as removing items from the Dock, using the System Preferences, changing passwords, burning CDs or DVDs, and even restricting which applications and utilities are available to the user.

Classic

> Use this to start, stop, and restart the Classic environment. For additional information, see "Mac OS X and the Classic Environment," earlier in this book.

Date & Time

> This panel is used to set the date and time for your system, as well as your time zone, specify a network time server, and how (or whether) the date and time will appear in the menu bar.

Software Update

> As with Mac OS 9, the Software Update panel can be used to check for updates to your Mac OS X system. You can use this panel to check for updates manually (i.e., when you want to, or when you learn of an available update) or automatically (daily, weekly, or monthly). When an update is found, you will be prompted to specify which updates will be downloaded and installed on your system.

Speech

> This panel can be used to turn on and configure speech recognition, to specify a default voice for applications

that speak text, and to specify whether items in the user interface (such as alert messages or the text in menus) will be spoken as well.

Startup Disk

This panel is used to specify whether your system will boot into Mac OS 9 or Mac OS X. With Jaguar, you can also specify a Network Startup disk if your computer is configured or set up via NetBoot from Mac OS X Server.

Universal Access

The Universal Access panel provides support for people with disabilities. Jaguar features two panes for people who have problems Seeing or Hearing, and includes two additional panes for those who find it difficult to use a Keyboard or Mouse.

One thing you'll quickly notice is that all the text labels for the user interface elements in the Universal Access panel are spoken using the voice you've specified in the Speech panel.

After you've completed tweaking your System Preferences, use ⌘-Q to Quit the application.

Applications and Utilities

Apple has included a set of native applications and utilities for Mac OS X, including the famous iApps (iMovie, iPhoto, and iTunes; future releases will most likely include iCal and iSync as well).

There are applications for such things as viewing and printing PDF files, basic word processing, sending and receiving email, and creating movies, as well as utilities to help you manage your system.

Use the Finder to locate the Applications (*/Applications*) and Utilities (*/Applications/Utilities*) on your system. You can quickly go to the *Applications* folder either by clicking on the

Applications icon in the toolbar or by using the Shift-⌘-A keyboard shortcut. Because there is no keyboard shortcut to the Utilities, you might consider dragging the Utilities folder icon to the Finder toolbar.

Applications

The following is a list of the programs found in the *Applications* directory:

Acrobat Reader
> This is Adobe Systems' application for viewing and printing PDF files.

Address Book
> This is a database program you can use to store contact information for your friends and colleagues.

AppleScript
> This folder contains all the tools necessary for writing AppleScripts. If you've downloaded or installed the Developer Tools (see the section "Developer Tools"), you will also have the ability to build applications using AppleScript Studio.

Calculator
> The Calculator application that ships with Jaguar has a fully-functional scientific calculator, compared to the simple four function one that shipped with earlier versions of the Mac OS. Calculator also has a Paper Tape sheet that allows you to view the math functions, which you can copy and paste into another application.

Chess
> Based on GNU Chess, Apple has taken this Unix-based chess game and packaged it with a Cocoa interface and 3D game pieces.

Clock
> Launching this application places a Clock icon in the Dock. By changing the Clock's preferences, you can

switch the display from analog to digital, display the time in 24-hour format (military time), and set the clock to be a floating window on the desktop.

DVD Player

If your hardware natively supports DVD playback, the DVD Player will be installed. You can use this application to view DVD movies on your Mac.

iCal

iCal is a calendaring application (similar to Entourage, if you're a Windows convert), which allows you to manage and publish your calendar to any WebDAV-enabled server (including your .Mac account). You can also subscribe to other calendars (such as a listing of holidays, the schedule for your favorite sports team, or that of another user). iCal didn't release in time to make it on the CDs for Jaguar; however, you can download it from Apple at *http://www.apple.com/ical*.

iChat

This is the new chat client. iChat allows you to chat with other .Mac members, as well as with AOL Instant Messenger (AIM) users. iChat also supports messaging via Rendezvous, for dynamically finding iChat users on your local network. To learn more about iChat, go to Apple's page at *http://www.apple.com/macosx/jaguar/ichat.html*.

Image Capture

This program can be used to download pictures and video from a digital camera to your Mac.

iMovie

Use iMovie to create digital movies on your Mac. To learn more about iMovie, see *iMovie 2: The Missing Manual* (Pogue Press/O'Reilly), or go to Apple's page at *http://www.apple.com/imovie*.

Internet Connect

This application is used for connecting to the Internet or to another computer via a dial-up modem or an AirPort connection. New with Jaguar, you can use Internet Connect to get connected to a Virtual Private Network (VPN) via File → New VPN Connection Window.

Internet Connect shows your current dial-up status and settings (as configured in the Network pane of your System Preferences) and provides a Connect/Disconnect button for opening or closing a connection.

Internet Explorer

Microsoft's Internet Explorer 5.2.1 is Mac OS X's default web browser.

iPhoto

iPhoto allows you to download, organize, and edit images taken with a digital camera. iPhoto is much more powerful than Image Capture, described earlier. To learn more about iPhoto, see *iPhoto: The Missing Manual* (Pogue Press/O'Reilly), or Apple's iPhoto page at *http://www.apple.com/iphoto*.

iSync

iSync can be used to synchronize data—contact information from your Address Book, your iCal calendars, music, etc.—from your computer to another device such as a cellular phone, PDA, iPod, or another computer. iSync is a late addition to Jaguar and is available for download from Apple's web site at *http://www.apple.com/isync*.

iTunes

iTunes can be used to play CDs, listen to Internet radio stations, import (rip) music from CDs, burn CDs from music you've collected, and store and play MP3 files. If you have an iPod, you can also use iTunes to synchronize your MP3 music files. To learn more about iTunes, see Apple's page at *http://www.apple.com/itunes*.

Mail

This is the default email client for Mac OS X.

Preview

Preview is a simple image viewer that lets you open (and export) files that have been saved in a variety of image formats, including PICT, GIF, JPEG, and TIFF, to name a few. Preview can also be used for opening and viewing PDF files, the standard format now for the screenshots you create with Shift-⌘-3 or Shift-⌘-4.

QuickTime Player

This is used for playing QuickTime movies, as well as listening to QuickTime streaming audio and video.

Sherlock

Unlike previous versions of Sherlock, which you could use to index and search for items on your system, Sherlock 3 is Apple's venture into web services. (As mentioned earlier, the search functionality has been built into the Finder, and indexing is done via the Get Info window for drives, partitions, and folders.) To use Sherlock under Jaguar, you *must* have a connection to the Internet. Sherlock 3 can be used to conduct searches on the Internet for:

- Pictures
- Stock quotes
- Movie theaters and show times
- Locating a business in your area (based on the address information you provide in Sherlock's preferences), along with driving directions and a map to the location
- Bidding on eBay auction items
- Checking the arrival and departure times of airline flights
- Finding the definition or spelling for a word in the dictionary

- Searching in AppleCare's Knowledge Base to solve a problem you're having with your computer
- Getting a quick translation from one language to another

Stickies

Stickies is a simple application that lets you create sticky notes on your screen. Like the notes stuck to your desk or computer, Stickies can be used to store important notes and reminders.

System Preferences

This is the System Preferences application, described earlier and throughout this book.

TextEdit

Like most applications that come with Jaguar, TextEdit also received a bit of an upgrade. TextEdit now sports a ruler bar with text formatting buttons for changing the alignment, leading, and indentation of text. By default, TextEdit documents are saved as rich text format (*.rtf* and *.rtfd*), but you can also save documents as plain text (*.txt*) via the Format → Make Plain Text menu option. TextEdit replaces the SimpleText application from earlier versions of the Mac OS.

Utilities

The tools found in the Utilities folder can be used to help you manage your Mac:

AirPort Admin Utility

This utility is used to administer AirPort Base Stations.

AirPort Setup Assistant

This utility is used for configuring your system to connect to an AirPort wireless network.

Apple System Profiler

The Apple System Profiler keeps track of the finer details about your system. Here, you can view information about your particular computer, the devices (e.g., Zip or Jaz drive, CD-ROM drives, etc.) and volumes (i.e., hard drives and partitions) connected to your Mac, as well as listings of the frameworks, extensions, and applications on your Mac.

Audio MIDI Setup

This utility is used to add, set up, and configure Musical Instrument Digital Interface (MIDI) devices connected to your Mac.

Bluetooth File Exchange

This utility allows you to exchange files with other Bluetooth-enabled devices, such as cellular phones, PDAs, and other computers. To exchange a file, launch this utility and then drag a file from the Finder to the Bluetooth File Exchange icon in the Dock. A window will appear, asking you to select a recipient (or recipients) for the file.

ColorSync Utility

This utility has three significant features. By pressing the Profile First Aid icon, it can be used to verify and repair your ColorSync settings. The Profiles icon keeps track of the ColorSync profiles for your system, and the Devices icon lets you see which ColorSync devices are connected, as well as the name and location of the current profile.

Console

The primary use of the Console application is to log the interactions between applications on your system and also with the operating system itself. If you enable crash logging (Console → Preferences → Crashes), the Console will open automatically when an application quits unexpectedly. The crash log created by the Console application can be used by developers to help debug their applications.

CPU Monitor

This is a simple meter that shows you the current load on your Mac's processor. If you have a dual-processor machine, there will be two meters.

DigitalColor Meter
> The DigitalColor Meter is a small application that lets you view and copy the color settings for any pixel on your screen.

Directory Access
> This utility controls access for Mac OS X systems to Directory Services, such as NetInfo, LDAP, and Active Directory.

Disk Copy
> This is a useful tool for creating disk images (*.dmg*) for batching up and sending files (including folders and applications) from one Mac user to another.

Disk Utility
> This utility can be used to repair a damaged hard drive, as well as for initializing and partitioning new drives.

Display Calibrator
> This helps you calibrate your display to create a custom ColorSync profile.

Grab
> The Grab utility can be used to take screenshots of your system. Two of its most useful features include the ability to select the pointer (or no pointer at all) to be displayed in the screenshot, as well as the ability to start a 10-second timer before the screenshot is taken to give you the necessary time to set up the shot.

Installer
> This program launches whenever you install an application on your system.

Java
> The following Java utilities can be found in this directory:

> *Applet Launcher*
> > This utility lets you run Java applets on your Mac.

Java Plugin Settings

This controls Java settings when Java is run in a browser.

Java Web Start

Java Web Start (or JWS) can be used to download and run Java applications.

Key Caps

Key Caps can be used to view the characters available for any font on your system. Different fonts contain different hidden characters; you can select a different font using the Fonts menu. See Table 21 in "Special Characters" for a listing of the keyboard shortcuts for creating special and international characters.

Keychain Access

This utility can be used to create and manage your passwords for accessing secure web and FTP sites, networked filesystems, and other items such as password-encoded files.

NetInfo Manager

The NetInfo Manager is mainly a tool for system and network administrators to view and edit the settings for a system. You need to have administrator privileges to use NetInfo Manager.

Network Utility

This utility is a graphical frontend to a standard set of Unix tools such as *netstat*, *ping*, *traceroute*, *whois*, and *finger*; it also lets you view specific information about your network connection and scan the available ports for a particular domain or IP address.

ODBC Administrator

A tool that allows you to connect to and exchange data with ODBC-compliant data sources. ODBC, which stands for Open Database Connectivity, is a standard database protocol, supported by most database systems such as FileMaker Pro, Oracle, MySQL, and Postgre-SQL. You can use ODBC Administrator to add data sources, install new database drivers, trace calls to the ODBC API, and configure connection pooling.

Print Center

The Print Center is the utility that configures and controls the printers connected to your computer, either locally or on a network via AppleTalk, Directory Services (via IP or Rendezvous), IP Printing, or USB. For users who are coming over from Mac OS 9, the Print Center replaces the Chooser for managing printers.

Process Viewer

This program lets you view the processes running on your system. If you click on a process name, you can see additional information about that process by clicking on the disclosure triangle next to "More Info," or you can cancel (*kill*, in Unix-speak) by highlighting a process and choosing Processes → Quit Process (Shift-⌘-Q).

StuffIt Expander

StuffIt Expander is the popular utility for expanding, or decompressing, files. To launch StuffIt Expander, simply double-click on the compressed file. StuffIt Expander can open files saved as *.bin*, *.hqx*, *.sit*, *.zip*, *.tar*, *.tar.gz*, and *.tgz*, to name a few.

Terminal

The Terminal application is the command-line interface (CLI) to Mac OS X's Unix core. For more information about the Terminal, see "System Preferences," later in this book.

Developer Tools

Apple has gone to great lengths to lure a new breed of developers to the Mac, offering environments for traditional C, C++, Objective-C (and recently Objective-C++), Java, Perl,

Python, Ruby, and with the introduction of AppleScript Studio, AppleScripters can now harness their scripting knowledge to build Cocoa-based applications.

Installing the Developer Tools

You can quickly check to see if you have the Developer Tools installed. If you have a */Developer* folder on your hard drive, you are ready to go. If not, you'll need to install the tools either from the Developer Tools CD that came with your system or from a disk image you can download from the Apple Developer Connection (ADC) site.

The Developer Tools CD comes with every boxed set of Mac OS X (including Mac OS X Server), as well as with new Macs shipped from the factory with OS X. To install the tools, simply find the CD (it's the gray one), put it into your CD-ROM drive, and double-click the *Developer.mpkg* file that appears.

NOTE

If you didn't receive a Developer Tools CD with your new Mac, you can find *Developer.mpkg* in */Applications/ Installers/Developer Tools*.

If you can't find your Developer Tools CD, you should go to the ADC member web site at *http://connect.apple.com*, register as an online member (it's free), and then you can download the Developer Tools.

NOTE

There are many levels of ADC membership available. The free Online membership gets you a good range of benefits, including access to the latest version of the Developer Tools and the ability to track bugs that you submit. You can register a free for online membership at *http://connect.apple.com*.

To download the Tools, log in to the ADC Member web site, click on Download Software in the navigation bar, and then on the Mac OS X subcategory link that appears. From this page you can download the Developer Tools either in segments or in one big chunk. If you download the Tools in segments, simply double-click on the first segment, and StuffIt will launch and put all the segments together into one file.

The Tools are provided as a Disk Image (*.dmg*) file. When you double-click on a disk image, a temporary disk is mounted onto your system. Simply navigate to this disk in the Finder, and double-click on the *Developer.mpkg* file to launch the installer.

Overview of the Developer Tools

As noted in the previous section, the Developer Tools are installed in the */Developer/Applications* directory on your system. This section will briefly describe the more commonly used Tools:

Interface Builder
> Interface Builder is a GUI editor for both Cocoa and Carbon applications. It has complete online help and release notes, available by launching Project Builder and using the Help menu.

Project Builder
> Project Builder is an integrated development environment for Mac OS X. It supports both Cocoa and Carbon, using C, C++, Objective-C, and Java. It has complete online help and release notes, available by launching Project Builder and using the Help menu.

FileMerge
> FileMerge compares two files or directories and lets you merge them together.

PackageManager

PackageManager lets you package your software so that the Mac OS X Installer can install it on a user's machine.

icns Browser

The icns Browser is used to display the contents of a *.icns* file.

IconComposer

IconComposer is used to create icon files (*.icns*) from existing images.

PEFViewer

PEFViewer displays the contents of a PEF binary as a hexadecimal dump.

Pixie

Pixie displays a magnified image of whatever is under the mouse.

Property List Editor

The Property List Editor lets you edit and create XML property lists.

For additional information about other development tools, including command-line and Java tools, see */Developer/ Documentation/DeveloperTools/DevToolsOverview.html*.

PART IV

Mac OS X Unix Basics

This part is a basic introduction to show new users the Unix side of Mac OS X. Specifically, this section will cover:

- Configuring and using the Terminal
- Command-line editing with *tcsh*
- Additional shell commands, such as *bindkey*, *defaults*, and *open*
- Basic Unix commands

You don't *have* to venture into the command line if you don't want to, but it's easy to be seduced by its power, as this part shows you a glimpse at what's possible with just a few easy keystrokes.

Configuring and Using the Terminal

The Terminal application (*/Applications/Utilities*) is your interface to Mac OS X's Unix shell. The Terminal can be used for everything from creating new directories (folders) and files to launching applications, and from managing and monitoring your system to programming and tweaking your system preferences.

Terminal Settings

This section offers advice on how to configure the settings for your Terminal. Previously, you would use Terminal →

Preferences to configure the Terminal's settings. However, with Jaguar, you'll need to use File → Show Info and change the settings from the Terminal Inspector window via the pull-down menu at the top of the window.

Change the style of the cursor?
  Display & Cursor Style → (Block, Underline, Vertical Bar).

Stop the cursor from blinking?
  Display → Cursor Style → Deselect Blinking Cursor.

Change the background color and font colors of the Terminal window?
  Color → click on the color selection boxes next to Background, Cursor, Normal Text, Bold Text, and Selection to open another window with the color wheel, which allows you to change and select a different color and even the transparency of the Terminal window.

Assign a different title to the Terminal window?
  Window → Title.

Assign a different title to the current Terminal window?
  With an open Terminal window, select File → Set Title (Shift-⌘-T). The Terminal Inspector window will open with Window selected in the pull-down menu. Enter a new title for the window in the Title field and hit Return or Tab to change the title of the current window.

Specify the number of lines a Terminal window can contain in the scrollback buffer?
  Buffer → Buffer Size. You can either specify a number of lines in the field provided (10,000 lines is the default), or select from an unlimited scrollback or no scrollback at all.

Set the Terminal's emulation mode to VT100?
  Emulation → Strict VT-100 keypad behavior.

Close the Terminal window after I've exited?
  Shell → When the shell exits → (select from either "Close the window" or "Close only if the shell exited cleanly").

Where is the history file for the shell?

It's located in your home directory as *.tcsh_history*. The history file keeps track of recently entered commands, which you can recall in a variety of ways, the easiest of which is to use the Up or Down Arrows to go back or forward in the history file, respectively.

Where is the shell's configuration file located?

In */usr/share/tcsh/examples/rc*.

Can I create a customized shell environment that's different from the one used by other users on the system?

Yes, but read and follow the instructions in the *README* file located in */usr/share/tcsh/examples*.

Keyboard Shortcuts

Table 8 lists the keyboard shortcuts that can be used with the Terminal application.

Table 8. Keyboard shortcuts for use with the Terminal

Key command	Description
⌘-. (period)	Terminate process (same as Control-C, the Unix interrupt command)
⌘-Up Arrow	Scrolls up one line at a time
⌘-Down Arrow	Scroll down one line at a time
⌘-Left Arrow	Go to previous Terminal window
⌘-Right Arrow	Go to next Terminal window
FN-Up Arrow	Scroll up one screen at a time
FN-Down Arrow	Scroll down one screen at a time
FN-Left Arrow	Scroll backward to the top of the screen
FN-Right Arrow	Scroll forward to the bottom of the screen
⌘-A	Select all the text in the Terminal window, including the scrollback
Shift-⌘-C	Use to open or close the Colors window

Table 8. Keyboard shortcuts for use with the Terminal (continued)

Key command	Description
⌘-I	Open the Terminal Inspector, which allows you to change some of the Terminal's settings
⌘-K	Clear all the information from the Terminal window, disabling scrollback (this is different and more extensive than the *clear* command, described later)
⌘-N	Open new Terminal window
Shift-⌘-N	Run a command in a new Terminal window
⌘-S	Save the settings of the Terminal window as a *.term* file
Shift-⌘-S	Save the settings of the Terminal window as a differently named *.term* file
Option-⌘-S	Save the contents of the Terminal window, including any scrollback, as a text file
Shift-Option-⌘-S	Save any selected text in the Terminal window as a text file
⌘-T	Open the Font panel so you can change the Terminal's default font settings, including the font family, size, and color
⌘-*number*	Switch to a different Terminal window, based on its *number*

Command-Line Editing with tcsh

Mac OS X's default user shell, *tcsh*, lets you move your cursor around in the command line, editing the line as you type. There are two main modes for editing the command line, based on the two most commonly used text editors: Emacs and vi. Emacs mode is the default; you can switch between the modes with:

bindkey -e
  Select Emacs bindings

bindkey -v
  Select vi bindings

The main difference between the Emacs and vi bindings is that the Emacs bindings are modeless (i.e., they always work). With the vi bindings, you must switch between insert and command modes; different commands are useful in each mode. Additionally:

- Emacs mode is simpler; vi mode allows finer control.
- Emacs mode allows you to cut text and set a mark; vi mode does not.
- The command-history-searching capabilities differ.

Emacs Mode

Table 9 through Table 11 describe the various editing keystrokes available in Emacs mode.

Table 9. Cursor-positioning commands (Emacs mode)

Command	Description
Control-B	Move the cursor back (left) one character
Control-F	Move the cursor forward (right) one character
Esc-B	Move the cursor back one word
Esc-F	Move the cursor forward one word
Control-A	Move the cursor to the beginning of the line
Control-E	Move the cursor to the end of the line

Table 10. Text-deletion commands (Emacs mode)

Command	Description
Del or Control-H	Delete the character to the left of the cursor
Control-D	Delete the character under the cursor
Esc-D	Delete the next word
Esc-Delete or Esc-Control-H	Delete the previous word
Control-K	Delete from the cursor to the end of the line
Control-U	Delete the entire line

Table 11. Command control (Emacs mode)

Command	Description
Control-P or Up Arrow	Recall the previous command from history
Control-N or Down Arrow	Recall the next command from history
cmd-fragment Esc-P	Search history for cmd-fragment, which must be the beginning of a command
cmd-fragment Esc-N	Like Esc-P, but search forward in the history
Esc num	Repeat the next command num times
Control-Y	Yank the previously deleted string

vi Mode

vi mode has two submodes: insert mode and command mode. The default mode is insert. You can toggle between the modes by pressing Esc; alternatively, in command mode, typing **a** (append) or **i** (insert) will return you to insert mode.

Tables 12 through 18 describe the editing keystrokes available in vi mode.

Table 12. Commands available (vi Insert and Command mode)

Command	Description
Control-P or Up Arrow	Recall the previous command from history
Control-N or Down Arrow	Recall the next command from history

Table 13. Editing commands (vi Insert mode)

Command	Description
Control-B	Move the cursor back (left) one character
Control-F	Move the cursor forward (right) one character
Control-A	Move the cursor to the beginning of the line

Table 13. Editing commands (vi Insert mode) (continued)

Command	Description
Control-E	Move the cursor to the end of the line
Delete or Control-H	Delete the character to the left of the cursor
Control-W	Delete the previous word
Control-U	Delete from the beginning of the line to the cursor
Control-K	Delete from the cursor to the end of the line

Table 14. Cursor-positioning commands (vi Command mode)

Command	Description
h or Control-H	Move the cursor back (left) one character
l or Space	Move the cursor forward (right) one character
w	Move the cursor forward (right) one word
b	Move the cursor back (left) one word
e	Move the cursor to the ending of the next word
W, B, E	Like w, b, and e, but treat whitespace as a word separator instead of any nonalphanumeric character
^ or Control-A	Move the cursor to the beginning of the line (first nonwhitespace character)
0	Move the cursor to the beginning of the line
$ or Control-E	Move the cursor to the end of the line

Table 15. Text-insertion commands (vi Command mode)

Command	Description
a	Append new text after the cursor until Esc is pressed
i	Insert new text before the cursor until Esc is pressed
A	Append new text after the end of the line until Esc is pressed
I	Insert new text before the beginning of the line until Esc is pressed

Table 16. Text-deletion commands (vi Command mode)

Command	Description
x	Delete the character under the cursor
X or Delete	Delete the character to the left of the cursor
d*m*	Delete from the cursor to the end of motion command *m*
D	Deletes from the cursor to the end of the line (similar to issuing d$)
Control-W	Delete the previous word
Control-U	Delete from the beginning of the line up to the cursor
Control-K	Delete from the cursor to the end of the line

Table 17. Text-replacement commands (vi Command mode)

Command	Description
c*m*	Change the characters from the cursor to the end of motion command *m* until Esc is pressed
C	Changes the correct word to whatever you type (similar to issuing c$)
r*c*	Replace the character under the cursor with the character *c*
R	Replace multiple characters until Esc is pressed
s	Substitute the character under the cursor with the characters typed until Esc is pressed

Table 18. Character-seeking motion commands (vi Command mode)

Command	Description
f*c*	Move the cursor to the next instance of *c* in the line
F*c*	Move the cursor to the previous instance of *c* in the line
t*c*	Move the cursor just after the next instance of *c* in the line
T*c*	Move the cursor just after the previous instance of *c* in the line
;	Repeat the previous f or F command
,	Repeat the previous f or F command in the opposite direction

Additional Command-Line Keys

As was just illustrated, the *tcsh* shell offers dozens of special keystroke characters for navigation on the command line. Table 19 lists some additional command-line keys for use in either Emacs or vi editing mode.

Table 19. Additional key commands for the tcsh shell

Key command	Description
Control-C	Interrupt the process; cancels the previous command (⌘-. works as well).
Control-D	Used to signal end of input; will terminate most programs and return you to the shell prompt. If Control-D is issued at a shell prompt, it will close the Terminal window.
Control-I	Display an *ls*-style listing of a directory's contents; directories in the output will have a forward slash (/) after the directory name.
Control-J	Same as pressing the Return (or Enter) key; hitting Control-J after issuing a command invokes the command, or it takes you to the next line in the shell if no command was given.
Control-K	Remove everything to the right of the insertion point.
Control-L	Clear the display (same as typing *clear* and hitting Return).
Control-Q	Restart output after a pause by Control-S.
Control-S	Pause the output from a program that's writing to the screen.
Control-T	Transpose the previous two characters.
Control-Z	Suspend a process. To restart the process, issue the *bg* or *fg* command to place the process in the background or foreground, respectively.
Esc-C	Capitalize the word following the insertion point.
Esc-Esc	If only a partial path or filename is entered, pressing the Esc key twice will complete the name. (Pressing the Esc key twice is the same as the Tab key once.)
Esc-L	Change the next word to all lowercase letters.
Esc-U	Change the next word to all uppercase letters.
Tab	Has the same effect as pressing the Esc key twice.

Additional Shell Commands

One of the first things that traditional Unix users will notice when they start poking around in the Terminal is that there are a few new commands they'll need to add to their repertoire. Three that we'll discuss here are *bindkey*, *defaults*, and *open*.

bindkey

bindkey is a *tcsh* shell command, used to select, examine, and define key bindings for use in the Terminal. Table 20 shows the various uses of the *bindkey* command.

Table 20. Using the bindkey command

Command	Description
bindkey	List all the key bindings
bindkey -c key cmd	Bind *key* to Unix command *cmd*
bindkey -d	Restore the default key bindings
bindkey -e	Change the key bindings to Emacs mode
bindkey *key*	List the bindings for *key*
bindkey key cmd	Bind *key* to editing command *cmd*
bindkey -l	List the editing commands and their meanings
bindkey -r key	Remove binding for *key*
bindkey -s key str	Bind *key* to string *str*
bindkey -u	Display a message, showing how to use the *bindkey* command
bindkey -v	Change the key bindings to vi mode

For additional information on key bindings and how to alter them, see *Using csh & tcsh* (O'Reilly).

defaults

When you customize your Mac using the System Preferences, or an application's preferences, all those changes and settings are stored in what's known as the *preferences system*, and the command-line utility to change your preferences is the *defaults* command. Everything that you've done to make your Mac yours is stored as XML data in the form of a *property list* (or *plist*). Your property lists are stored in *~/Library/Preferences*.

WARNING

Using the *defaults* command is not for the foolhardy. If you're not comfortable with the command line or unsure of how to change a setting properly, you should stick to using the application's Preferences pane, rather than trying to use the *defaults* command.

If you do manage to mangle your settings, the easiest way to correct the problem is to go back to that application's Preferences pane and reset your preferences. Another solution is to delete the preferences file for the application from *~/Library/Preferences*.

Every time you change one of those settings, that particular property list is updated. For the initiated, there are two other ways to alter the property lists. The first is by using the Property List Editor application (*/Developer/Applications*), and the other is by using the *defaults* command in the Terminal. Extensive coverage of both is beyond the scope of this book, but we'll show you a few basic examples of how to use the *defaults* command.

Examples

The following are some examples of working with the *defaults* command:

View all the user defaults on your system
```
% defaults domains
```

This will print a listing of all the *domains* in the user's defaults system. The lists you'll see are run together with spaces in between—not quite the prettiest way to view them.

View the settings for your Dock

```
% defaults read com.apple.dock
```

This command reads the settings from the *com.apple. dock.plist* file, found in *~/Library/Preferences*. This listing is rather long, so you might want to pipe the output to *less* or *more* to view the contents one screen at a time:

```
% defaults read com.apple.dock | more
```

Change the location of your Dock to the top of the screen

Near the beginning of that listing, look for the following:

```
orientation = bottom;
```

You'll see that its value is set to bottom, which means that your Dock is located at the bottom of the screen. To change that setting, try the following:

```
% defaults write com.apple.dock orientation top
```

After a short pause, you'll be returned to another command prompt, but you'll notice that the Dock is still located at the bottom of the screen. Unlike some other changes you make with the *defaults* command, changes to the Dock will take effect only if you log out and log back in.

Enter *exit*, and quit the Terminal, and then save any changes in other applications and quit them too. Now log out and log back in to your system (Apple → Log Out). When you log back in, you'll see the Dock in all its glory floating just below the menu bar at the top of the screen. To quickly change its location back to the bottom of the screen (or the left or right side), use Apple → Dock → Position on (Left, Bottom, or Right).

For additional options and to learn more about how to use the *defaults* command, enter *defaults –help* or view the defaults manpage (*man defaults*).

open

With Mac OS X, you can launch any application from the command line using the *open* command. There are three ways to invoke the command:

open [*filename*]

> This will open the file and its associated application if it isn't already running. For example:

```
% open textFile.txt
```

> opens the file *textFile.txt* using the default text editor, which is TextEdit.

open -a [*application_path*] [*filename*]

> The *–a* option lets you specify the application to use when opening the file. For example, let's say you have both Microsoft Office 2001 and Office v.X on your system and you want to open a Word file using Word 2001. If you use open *filename.doc*, Word v.X will launch. To open the file with Word 2001, you need to do the following:

```
% open -a /Volumes/Mac\ OS\ 9/Applications\ \(Mac\ ↵
OS\ 9\)/Microsoft\ Office\ 2001/Microsoft\ Word ↵
~/Documents/filename.doc
```

> While that might look ugly (and it is), the command does work. In this case, Classic would also launch because Word 2001 is a Classic app.

NOTE

There is a shortcut for inserting long pathnames like the one shown in this example: locate the application in the Finder, and drag the application icon from the Finder window to the Terminal window after typing *open –a* at the command line. The path for the application will be inserted after the command, and then you need only tack on the path and filename for the file.

```
open -e [filename_path]
```
The *–e* option forces the use of the TextEdit application.
For example:

```
% open -e ~/Books/Templates/proposal_template.txt
```

Some additional examples of using the Terminal to open files
and launch applications are shown here:

*Open an HTML page using a browser other than Internet
Explorer?*

The other way to do this is to specify the application,
using the *–a* option:

```
% open -a /Applications/Navigator.app Sites/index.html
```

The *–a* option is used to launch Chimera, the Cocoa-com-
pliant web browser, which is based on the Mozilla source
code (hence its true application name, Navigator) for Mac
OS X (assuming you have Chimera installed on your system, *http://www.mozilla.org/projects/chimera*) for viewing
the *index.html* file, located in your Sites directory.

Launch Classic from the Terminal?

If you find that you're using the Classic environment,
one way you can launch Classic from the Terminal is
with the following:

```
% open /System/Library/CoreServices/Classic\ ↵
Startup.app
```

And while that does the trick, a faster way to do this is to
set up an *alias* in the shell. To do this, enter the following on the command line:

```
% alias classic 'open -a /System/Library/ ↵
CoreServices/ Classic\ Startup.app'
```

Now to launch the Classic environment, simply type
classic on the command line and hit return.

This assumes you're running *tcsh* as the default shell. If
you're running *bash*, use the following to set up the
classic alias:

```
$ alias classic='open -a /System/Library/ ↵
CoreServices/Classic\ Startup.app'
```

Basic Unix Commands

If you've never used Unix before, this section will serve as a quick introduction to issuing Unix commands from the Terminal. Experienced Unix users can skip over this section. For each of the following, you will need to be using the Terminal application. The commands you need to type are shown in bold.

View a command's description and its options?

All the Unix commands on your system have a manual page (or *manpage* for short). To view the manpage for any command, you use the *man* command:

```
[macchuck:~] chuck% man pwd
```

The instructions for using the *pwd* command (described next) are then displayed one screen at a time. If there is more than one screen for a command's description, you will see a percentage at the lower-left corner of the Terminal window telling you how much of the manpage has been viewed. To scroll to the next screen, hit the spacebar; you will be returned to the command prompt when you've reached the end of the manpage. The *man* command even has its own manpage, which can be viewed by using:

```
[macchuck:~] chuck% man man
```

Where am I?

Type *pwd* on the command line, and hit Return; this will tell you the present working directory.

```
[macchuck:~] chuck% pwd
/Users/chuck
[macchuck:~] chuck%
```

The default *tcsh* command prompt will show you what directory you're in, but only to a point; for example:

```
[macchuck:Applications/Extras/Bluetooth] chuck% pwd
/Developer/Applications/Extras/Bluetooth
[macchuck:Applications/Extras/Bluetooth] chuck%
```

As this example shows, at first it only looks like I'm in *Applications/Extras/Bluetooth*, but issuing the *pwd* command shows that I'm really in */Developer/Applications/ Extras/Bluetooth*. Your cue that you are in a deeper path is that there is no slash before the first directory in the prompt.

Change directories?

Use the *cd* command and go to the Utilities directory:

```
[macchuck:~] chuck% cd /Applications/Utilities
[macchuck:/Applications/Utilities] chuck%
```

Go back a directory?

Use the *cd* command followed by two dots:

```
[macchuck:/Applications/Utilities] chuck% cd ..
[macchuck:/Applications] chuck%
```

Return to where you were before the last cd command?

Use the *cd* command followed by a hyphen:

```
[macchuck:/Applications] chuck% cd -
[macchuck:/Applications/Utilities] chuck%
```

Go back one or more directories?

Use the *cd* command with two dots and a slash (*../*) for each directory you want to go back. For example, to go back two directories:

```
[macchuck:/Applications/Utilities] chuck% cd ../..
[macchuck:/] chuck%
```

List a directory's contents?

This is accomplished using the *ls* command (see Figure 13).

By itself, the *ls* command creates a horizontal list of a directory's contents. Add the *–l* option to create a vertical list of a directory's contents, which also reveals more details about the file, directory, or application (see Figure 14).

To list all the contents for a directory, including the dot files (described earlier), add the *–a* option (either with or without the *l* option) (see Figure 15).

Figure 13. Listing a directory's contents with ls

```
000              Chuck's Term — tcsh (ttyp1)
[macchuck:/Applications/Utilities] chuck% ls -l
total 0
drwxrwxr-x  3 root  admin  102 Jul 29 04:16 AirPort Admin Utility.app
drwxrwxr-x  3 root  admin  102 Jul 29 04:27 AirPort Setup Assistant.app
drwxrwxr-x  3 root  admin  102 Jul 29 04:04 Apple System Profiler.app
drwxrwxr-x  7 root  admin  238 Jul 29 04:26 Asia Text Extras
drwxrwxr-x  3 root  admin  102 Jul 29 04:04 Audio MIDI Setup.app
drwxrwxr-x  3 root  admin  102 Jul 29 04:09 Bluetooth File Exchange.app
drwxrwxr-x  3 root  admin  102 Jul 29 04:04 CPU Monitor.app
drwxrwxr-x  3 root  admin  102 Jul 29 04:21 ColorSync Utility.app
drwxrwxr-x  3 root  admin  102 Jul 29 04:02 Console.app
drwxrwxr-x  3 root  admin  102 Jul 29 04:17 DigitalColor Meter.app
drwxrwxr-x  3 root  admin  102 Jun 13 21:35 Directory Access.app
drwxrwxr-x  3 root  admin  102 Jul 29 04:01 Disk Copy.app
drwxrwxr-x  3 root  admin  102 Jul 29 04:14 Disk Utility.app
drwxrwxr-x  3 root  admin  102 Jul 29 04:21 Display Calibrator.app
drwxrwxr-x  3 root  admin  102 Jul 29 04:03 Grab.app
drwxrwxr-x  3 root  admin  102 Sep 18 12:05 Installer.app
drwxrwxr-x  5 root  admin  170 Jul 27 23:40 Java
drwxrwxr-x  3 root  admin  102 Jul 29 04:13 Key Caps.app
drwxrwxr-x  3 root  admin  102 Jul 29 04:21 Keychain Access.app
drwxrwxr-x  3 root  admin  102 Jul 29 04:17 NetInfo Manager.app
drwxrwxr-x  3 root  admin  102 Jul 29 04:17 Network Utility.app
drwxrwxr-x  3 root  admin  102 Jul 29 04:03 ODBC Administrator.app
drwxrwxr-x  3 root  admin  102 Jul 29 04:16 Print Center.app
drwxrwxr-x  3 root  admin  102 Jul 29 04:13 Process Viewer.app
drwxrwxr-x  3 root  admin  102 Jul 27 04:01 StuffIt Expander.app
drwxrwxr-x  3 root  admin  102 Jul 29 04:05 Terminal.app
[macchuck:/Applications/Utilities] chuck%
```

Figure 14. Listing a directory's contents with ls –l

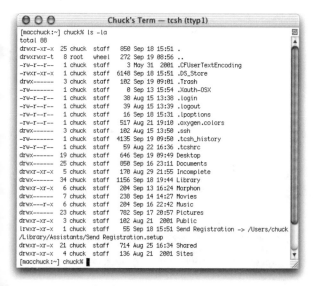

```
000              Chuck's Term — tcsh (ttyp1)
[macchuck:~] chuck% ls -la
total 88
drwxr-xr-x  25 chuck   staff    850 Sep 18 15:51 .
drwxrwxr-t   8 root    wheel    272 Sep 19 08:56 ..
-rw-r--r--   1 chuck   staff      3 May 31  2001 .CFUserTextEncoding
-rwxr-xr-x   1 chuck   staff   6148 Sep 18 15:51 .DS_Store
drwx------   3 chuck   staff    102 Sep 19 09:01 .Trash
-rw-------   1 chuck   staff      0 Sep 13 15:54 .Xauth-OSX
-rw-r--r--   1 chuck   staff     38 Aug 15 13:38 .login
-rw-r--r--   1 chuck   staff     39 Aug 15 13:39 .logout
-rw-r--r--   1 chuck   staff     16 Sep 18 15:31 .lpoptions
-rw-r--r--   1 chuck   staff    517 Aug 21 19:10 .oxygen.colors
drwx------   3 chuck   staff    102 Aug 15 13:50 .ssh
-rw-------   1 chuck   staff   4135 Sep 19 09:50 .tcsh_history
-rw-r--r--   1 chuck   staff     59 Aug 22 16:36 .tcshrc
drwx------  19 chuck   staff    646 Sep 19 09:49 Desktop
drwx------  25 chuck   staff    850 Sep 16 23:11 Documents
drwxr-xr-x   5 chuck   staff    170 Aug 29 21:55 Incomplete
drwx------  34 chuck   staff   1156 Sep 18 19:44 Library
drwxr-xr-x   6 chuck   staff    204 Sep 13 16:24 Morphon
drwx------   7 chuck   staff    238 Sep 14 14:27 Movies
drwx---r-x   6 chuck   staff    204 Sep 16 22:42 Music
drwx------  23 chuck   staff    782 Sep 17 20:57 Pictures
drwxr-xr-x   3 chuck   staff    102 Aug 21  2001 Public
lrwxr-xr-x   1 chuck   staff     55 Sep 18 15:51 Send Registration -> /Users/chuck
/Library/Assistants/Send Registration.setup
drwxr-xr-x  21 chuck   staff    714 Aug 25 16:34 Shared
drwxr-xr-x   4 chuck   staff    136 Aug 21  2001 Sites
[macchuck:~] chuck% █
```

Figure 15. Listing all a directory's contents—including dot files—
using ls –la

When you issue a command like *ls –la*, the contents of
some directories will scroll up, and you won't be able to
see everything. One solution to this is to just issue the
command and then use the Terminal window's scrollbar
to go back up. Or, more efficiently, pipe (|) the com-
mand to *more*, which will display the contents of the
directory one screen at a time (see Figure 16). The word
more will be highlighted at the bottom of the screen. To
go to the next screen, hit the spacebar; continue doing so
until you find the item you're looking for or until you
reach the end.

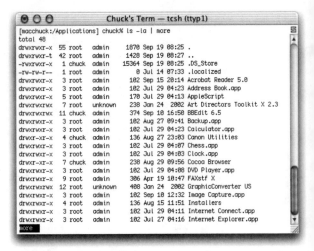

```
000                    Chuck's Term — tcsh (ttyp1)
[macchuck:/Applications] chuck% ls -la | more
total 48
drwxrwxr-x  55 root     admin        1870 Sep 19 08:25 .
drwxrwxr-t  42 root     admin        1428 Sep 19 08:27 ..
-rwxrwxr-x   1 chuck    admin       15364 Sep 19 08:25 .DS_Store
-rw-rw-r--   1 root     admin           0 Jul 14 07:33 .localized
drwxrwxr-x   3 root     admin         102 Sep 15 20:14 Acrobat Reader 5.0
drwxrwxr-x   3 root     admin         102 Jul 29 04:23 Address Book.app
drwxrwxr-x   5 root     admin         170 Jul 29 04:13 AppleScript
drwxrwxrwx   7 root     unknown       238 Jan 24  2002 Art Directors Toolkit X 2.3
drwxrwxrwx  11 chuck    admin         374 Sep 10 16:50 BBEdit 6.5
drwxrwxr-x   3 root     admin         102 Aug 27 09:41 Backup.app
drwxrwxr-x   3 root     admin         102 Jul 29 04:23 Calculator.app
drwxr-xr-x   4 chuck    admin         136 Aug 27 23:03 Canon Utilities
drwxrwxr-x   3 root     admin         102 Jul 29 04:07 Chess.app
drwxrwxr-x   3 root     admin         102 Jul 29 04:03 Clock.app
drwxr-xr-x   7 chuck    admin         238 Aug 29 09:56 Cocoa Browser
drwxrwxr-x   3 root     admin         102 Jul 29 04:08 DVD Player.app
drwxrwxr-x   9 root     admin         306 Apr 19 10:47 FAXstf X
drwxrwxrwx  12 root     unknown       408 Jan 24  2002 GraphicConverter US
drwxrwxr-x   3 root     admin         102 Sep 10 12:32 Image Capture.app
drwxrwxr-x   4 root     admin         136 Aug 15 11:51 Installers
drwxrwxr-x   3 root     admin         102 Jul 29 04:11 Internet Connect.app
drwxrwxr-x   3 root     admin         102 Jul 27 04:16 Internet Explorer.app
more
```

Figure 16. Listing a directory's contents with some assistance from the more command

How can I get a listing of a directory's contents without seeing the permissions?

Use *ls –l* and pipe the output of that listing to the *colrm* (column remove) command, as follows:

```
[macchuck:/Applications] chuck% ls -l | colrm 1 49

Acrobat Reader 5.0
Address Book.app
AppleScript
Art Directors Toolkit X 2.3
BBEdit 6.5
Backup.app
Calculator.app
Canon Utilities
Chess.app
Clock.app
Cocoa Browser
DVD Player.app
  .
  .
  .
```

The numbers following *colrm* (1 and 49) are used by the command to specify a range of columns to remove. (A column in the Unix world is a single character. In this example, the column range of 1 through 49—all the characters preceding the file or directory name—are deleted.)

Clear the display?

When you issue the *clear* command, the Terminal window scrolls down, placing the command prompt at the top of the display.

```
[macchuck:/Applications] chuck% clear
```

You can also use Control-L to clear the display, and if you want to reset the Terminal window, use ⌘-K to clear the window's scrollback.

Create a new directory (or folder)?

Use the *mkdir* command, followed by the name of the new directory you'd like to create:

```
[macchuck:~] chuck% mkdir NewDirectory
```

Remove an empty directory?

Use the *rmdir* command:

```
[macchuck:~] chuck% rmdir NewDirectory
```

Remove a directory and all its contents, including subdirectories?

Use the *rm* command with the *–rf* option to force the removal of the directory and its contents:

```
[macchuck:~] chuck% rm -rf NewDirectory
```

WARNING

Notice that the *rm –rf* command will not prompt you before it deletes everything in the *NewDirectory* directory. You should use the *rm –rf* command with extreme caution, as you could delete something vital without even knowing it.

Create an empty file?

There are many ways you can do this, but one of the easiest is by using the *touch* command:

```
[macchuck:~] chuck% touch myfile.txt
```

Copy a file or directory?

Use the *cp* command:

```
[macchuck:~] chuck% cp myfile.txt myfile2.txt
```

This makes a copy of *myfile.txt* and creates *myfile2.txt* within the same directory. If you want to copy a file and place it in another directory, use the following:

```
[macchuck:~] chuck% cp myfile.txt Books/myfile.txt
```

This makes a copy of *myfile.txt* and places that copy in the */Books* directory.

Rename a file or directory?

To rename a file, use the *mv* command:

```
[macchuck:~] chuck% mv myfile.txt myFile.txt
```

This renames the file *myfile.txt* to *myFile.txt* in the same directory.

Move a file or directory?

The following moves the file *myFile.txt* to the *Books* directory:

```
[macchuck:~] chuck% mv myFile.txt Books
```

See what's inside a file?

For this, you can use either *cat*, *more*, or *less*:

```
[macchuck:~/Books] chuck% cat myFile.txt
This is my file. I hope you like it.
Chuck
[macchuck:~/Books] chuck%
```

Make a file or directory read-only?

For this, you'll need to use the *chmod* (change mode) command. Any one of the following will assign read-only permission to *myFile.txt* for everyone:

```
[macchuck:~/Books] chuck% chmod =r myFile.txt
[macchuck:~/Books] chuck% chmod 444 myFile.txt
[macchuck:~/Books] chuck% chmod a-wx,a+r myFile.txt
```

The *chmod* command has many options; for more information, see its manpage (*man chmod*).

Zip up a file so I can send it to a Windows user?

To zip a file or directory, use the *zip* command, as follows:

```
[macchuck:~/Books] chuck% zip myFile.zip myFile.txt
```

This zips up the file and places the *myFile.zip* file in the same directory as the original file.

View the contents of a Zip file?

Use the *unzip* command with the *–l* option to list the contents of a Zip file, as follows:

```
[macchuck:~/Books] chuck% unzip -l myFile.zip
Archive:  myFile.zip
 Length    Date     Time    Name
 ------    ----     ----    ----
      0  09-18-102  20:20   myFile.txt
 ------                     -------
      0                     1 file
```

This shows that there is one file in *myFile.zip* (*myFile.txt*), along with the size of the file (in kilobytes), and the date and time that file was created.

Unzip a file that I received from a Windows user?

To unzip a file or directory, use the *unzip* command, as follows:

```
[macchuck:~/Books] chuck% unzip myFile.zip
```

This unzips the file and places its contents in the current directory. If a file with the same name is already in that directory, you will be asked what to do:

```
[macchuck:~/Books] chuck% unzip myFile.zip
Archive:  myFile.zip
replace myFile.txt? [y]es, [n]o, [A]ll, [N]one,
[r]ename: r
new name: myFile.txt.bak
 extracting: myFile2.txt
```

You will be given the following options to replace the existing file(s):

- **y** for yes
- **n** for no
- **A** to replace all the files with similar names
- **N** to *not* replace any of the files
- **r** to rename the like-named file that already exists

If you choose to rename the existing file (as shown in the example), you will be prompted to enter a new name for that file; enter a filename and that file's name will be changed and the *unzip* command will extract the Zip file.

Archive a file or directory?

To archive a file or directory, use the Unix tape archive command, *tar* , as follows:

```
[macchuck:~/Books] chuck% tar cvfz myFile.tar.gz ↵
myFile.txt
```

The options used are as follows:

c Creates a new archive.

v Verbose; this option prints the filenames onscreen as files that are added to or extracted from the archive.

f Stores files in or extract files from an archive.

z Uses *gzip* to zip, or compress, the archive.

View the contents of a tarball?

To peek inside a tarball to see the files it contains, use the *tar* command with the *tvfz* options:

```
[macchuck:~/Books] chuck% tar tvfz myFile.tar.gz
-rw-r--r--  1 chuck  staff  44 Oct 05 21:10 myFile.txt
```

The *–t* option is used to print the names of the files inside the tarball.

Open a .tar file?

To unpack a tarball (a *.tar* file), use the following:

```
[macchuck:~/Books] chuck% tar xvf myFile.tar ↵
myFile.txt
```

The *–x* option is used to extract the contents of the tarball. This command unpacks the tarball and places its contents in the file *myFile.txt*.

If you receive a *.tgz* (or *.tar.gz*) file, that means the tarball has been compressed using *gzip*. To decompress that file, use the following command:

```
[macchuck:~/Books] chuck% tar xvfz myFile.tgz ↵
myFile.txt
```

The *–z* option tells the *tar* command that the file it will decompress has been *gzip*'d.

Log in as the superuser?

Some commands require you to be the superuser (or the *root* user) before they can be issued. Rather than logging out and then logging back in as *root*, you can issue the *su* command, followed by the superuser's password:

```
[macchuck:~] chuck% su
Password: ********
[macchuck:/Users/chuck] root#
```

Now you have ultimate power—use it with great care as you could damage or overwrite something vital. When you are finished, issue the *exit* command to go back to being a normal user:

```
[macchuck:/Users/chuck] root# exit
exit
[macchuck:~] chuck%
```

NOTE

Remember, for most (if not all) tasks, you should be able to get by with using the *sudo* command instead of logging in as *root*.

For more information about using the Unix side of Mac OS X, pick up a copy of *Learning Unix for Mac OS X* (O'Reilly). To learn more about the *tcsh* shell, pick up a copy of *Using csh & tcsh* (O'Reilly).

PART V

Task and Setting Index

This final section of the book shows you how to configure and administer your Mac OS X system using the System Preferences and the Applications and Utilities that come with Mac OS X.

The book wraps up with a table that lists the special characters you can create from the keyboard.

Task and Setting Index

After rooting through all the System Preferences and looking at the Applications and Utilities that come with Mac OS X, you'll quickly find that there are literally hundreds of ways to configure the settings for your system. In some cases, instructions are provided for how to perform tasks using the GUI tools and by issuing Unix commands in the Terminal. Which is faster or easier to use is up to you to decide (but you're likely to realize quickly that the power of Unix is unmatchable by most GUI tools).

This section provides shorthand instructions to help you configure and use your Mac OS X system as quickly as possible. Each task is presented as the answer to a "How do I..." question (e.g., How do I change the color depth of my display?), followed by the shorthand way to execute the answer (e.g., System Preferences → Displays). The tasks are divided into the following ten categories:

- Customizing the System
- Files and Folders
- Fonts and Font Management
- Searching for and Locating Files
- Obtaining Information About the System
- Internet, Web, and Email
- Modems and Dial-Up Networking
- Networking
- Printer Configuration and Printing
- Maintenance and Troubleshooting

If you're new to Mac OS X, or if you just want to jog your memory when you can't quite remember where a particular setting is located, this is the place to start.

Customizing the System

The following are options you can use to customize the "Aqua look and feel" of your system:

Change my desktop size/resolution, or the color depth of my display?
> System Preferences → Displays → Display panel.

Change my Desktop image?
> System Preferences → Desktop.
>
> Control-click on the desktop itself and select Change Desktop Background from the context menu.

Have the pictures on my desktop change automatically?
> System Preferences → Desktop; click on the checkbox next to "Change picture" and select an interval from the pull-down menu.

Use one of the Mac OS 9 background images for my desktop instead of the (boring) ones that come with Mac OS X?
> System Preferences → Desktop → Collection → Choose Folder. A Finder sheet will slide down; use this to navi-

gate to Mac OS 9 System Folder → Appearance → Desktop Pictures. Then select one of the following folders, and click the Choose button: *3D Graphics*, *Convergency*, *Ensemble Photos*, or *Photos*. The images in that directory will appear as part of your Desktop Collection.

Add a new background pattern, making it available to all users?
    Create or save the image to either the *Abstract*, *Nature*, or *Solid Colors* folder in */Library/Desktop Pictures*.

Change the double-click speed of my mouse?
    System Preferences → Mouse → Mouse panel.

Change the scrolling speed for my scrollwheel mouse?
    System Preferences → Mouse → Mouse panel → Scrolling Speed.

Change the settings on my iBook's trackpad so it can emulate mouse clicks?
    System Preferences → Mouse → Trackpad panel → Use trackpad for (Clicking, Dragging, Drag Lock).

Change my login password?
    System Preferences → My Account; click on the Change button next to My Password.

    System Preferences → Accounts; double-click on your username to open the Edit User sheet and change your password.

    From the command line, use the *passwd* command.

Change the date/time?
    System Preferences → Date & Time → Date & Time panel.

Specify how the date and time will appear in the menu bar?
    System Preferences → Date & Time → Menu Bar Clock.

Specify the date and time settings for another country while I'm travelling?

To change the date: System Preferences → International → Date panel; select a country from the Region pull-down menu.

To change the time: System Preferences → International → Time panel; select a country from the Region pull-down menu.

Use a network time server to set my clock's time?

System Preferences → Date & Time → Network Time; click on the checkbox next to "Use a network time server" → select an NTP Server in the scroll list → click on the Set Time Now button

---

NOTE

You must be connected to the Internet to use a network time server. One helpful hint is to first use the network time server to set an accurate time for your system, then uncheck the "Use a network time server" box.

Set my time zone?

System Preferences → Date & Time → Time Zone. A map of the world will appear; simply click and drag the time zone bar to your location on the map, and let go of the mouse. As you move the time zone bar, the date and time in the menu bar change dynamically.

Display the current date and time from the command line?

Use the *date* command:

```
[macchuck:~] chuck% date
Wed Sep 18 20:33:43 EST 2002
```

Find out how long my system has been running?

Use the *uptime* command:

```
[macchuck:~] chuck% uptime
 8:34PM  up  10:09, 2 users, load averages: 0.09, ⏎
 0.12, 0.09
```

The *uptime* command displays, in the following order: the current time, how long the system has been running (*up 10:09*, or 10 hours 9 minutes), the number of users logged in to the system, and the load averages on the processor.

Change the name of my computer?
System Preferences → Sharing; enter the new name for your computer in the Computer Name text box.

Display the battery status for my PowerBook in the menu bar?
System Preferences → Energy Saver; select the checkbox next to "Show battery status in menu bar."

Display a volume control in the menu bar?
System Preferences → Sound; select the checkbox next to "Show volume in menu bar."

Automatically check for updates to the system?
System Preferences → Software Update → Update Software; select the checkbox next to "Automatically check for updates when you have a network connection," and then select the frequency (Daily, Weekly, Monthly) from the pull-down menu.

Have an application start up automatically after I log in?
System Preferences → Login Items panel. Click the Add button, and then use the Finder to select the applications you would like to have started after you log in.

Drag an application icon from the Finder to the window in the Login Items panel.

Adjust the amount of time my system needs to be idle before the screensaver kicks in?
System Preferences → Screen Effects → Activation.

Quickly activate my screensaver when I know I'll be away from my desk for a while?
System Preferences → Screen Effects → Hot Corners. Mark a corner of the screen with a check mark to activate the screen saver when the mouse is moved to that

corner. Likewise, you can place a minus sign in a Hot Corner to disable the screensaver when the mouse is moved there.

Protect my system from prying eyes while I'm away from my computer?

System Preferences → Screen Effects → Activation; select "Use my user account password" to require a password when waking the system from the screen saver.

Change the background of a window to a different color or to an image?

Finder → View → as Icons, then use View → Show View Options (⌘-J); select either Color or Picture for the Background option.

Restart my computer automatically after a power failure?

System Preferences → Energy Saver → Options pane; select the checkbox next to "Restart automatically after a power failure."

Enable full keyboard access so I can navigate through and select menu items without using a mouse?

System Preferences → Keyboard → Full Keyboard Access; select checkbox next to "Turn on full keyboard access."

Files and Folders

The following are options for use with files and folders:

Create a new folder?

Control-click → New Folder (in the Finder or on the Desktop).

Shift-⌘-N.

NOTE

In earlier versions of the Mac OS, ⌘-N was used to create new folders; now ⌘-N is used for opening a new Finder window.

Rename a file or folder?

Click once on the icon, and then click once on the name of the file to highlight it (or press Enter). Type in the new name for the file or folder, and hit return to accept the new name.

Click on the icon, and then use ⌘-I to open the Get Info window. Click on the disclosure triangle next to Name & Extension, and enter the new file or directory name.

In the Terminal, use the following command:

```
[macchuck:~] chuck% mv myFile.txt yourFile.txt
```

The *mv* command will change the name of *myFile.txt* to *yourFile.txt*.

Change the program associated with a particular extension?

Click on a file, and then use ⌘-I or File → Get Info. Click on the disclosure triangle next to "Open with" and select one of the applications from the pull-down menu, or choose Other to select a different program. If you want to specify that application as the default for opening files with that particular extension, click Change All; otherwise, close the Info window to save the changes.

Change the permissions for a file or directory?

Click on a file or directory, and then use ⌘-I or File → Get Info. Click on the disclosure triangle next to "Ownership & Privileges" to change the access for the Owner, Group, and Others.

Use the *chmod* command. To learn more about *chmod* and its options, see its manpage (*man chmod*).

Copy a file to the desktop instead of moving it or creating a shortcut?

Select the file, then Option-drag the icon to the Desktop (notice a plus sign will appear next to the pointer in a green bubble), and release the mouse button.

In the Finder, select the file → Edit → Copy *filename* →
Home → double-click on the Desktop icon → Edit →
Paste item.

Find out where an open document is saved on my system?

Command-click on the name of the document in the title
bar. A menu will drop down from the name of the file,
showing you where the file is located. If you pull down to
one of the folders in that menu and release the mouse, a
Finder window will open for that location.

How can I create a disk image?

Launch Disk Copy (*/Applications/Utilities*), then go to
File → New → Blank Image (⌘-N). Enter a name for the
disk image in the "Save as" field (a *.dmg* extension will be
appended), select where you would like it saved to, enter
a name for the volume, its size and format, and choose
whether the disk image will be encrypted. Click the Create button to create the disk image, which will be
mounted on your desktop. Double-click on the disk
image to open its Finder window, then drag and drop the
items you would like included in the disk image, close
the Finder window, and Eject the image (⌘-E) to com-
plete the process.

To create a disk image from an actual disk, such as your
hard drive or a CD, choose File → New → Image from
Device (Option-⌘-I) or Image from Folder or Volume
(⌘-I). Specify the details for the disk image and where
you would like it to be saved, and then click the Image
button.

*Display the contents of a shared folder on another volume in
my network?*

Finder → *volume* → *folder*.

From your home directory in the Terminal:

```
[macchuck:~] chuck% ls -la /Volumes/volume/folder
```

Quickly create a directory and a set of numbered directories (such as for chapters in a book)?

```
[macchuck:~] chuck% mkdir -p NewBook/ ⏎
{ch}{01,02,03,04,05}
[macchuck:~] chuck% ls -F NewBook
ch01/  ch02/  ch03/  ch04/  ch05/
```

Try doing that in the Finder—you can't! The first command, *ls –F NewBook* is used to list the folders within the *NewBook* directory, which shows us that five separate subdirectories have been created.

Quickly delete a directory (and its subdirectories) without sending it to Trash?

```
[macchuck:~] chuck% rm -rf work
```

Make the Trash stop asking me if I'm sure I want to delete every file?

Finder → Preferences; uncheck the option next to "Show warning before emptying the Trash."

Empty the trash of locked items?

Shift-Option-⌘-Delete. The addition of the Option key forces the deletion of the contents of Trash.

Give a file or folder a custom icon?

Open an image file, and copy it with ⌘-C. Select the icon → File → Get Info (or ⌘-I). Select the file icon in the General section, and then paste (⌘-V) in the new image.

NOTE

The proper image size for an icon is 128×128 pixels.

Fonts and Font Management

Use the following options for fonts and font management:

How can I share fonts with other users on my system?

If you're the administrator, move the font you'd like to share from your */Users/username/Library/Fonts* folder to */Library/Fonts*.

Where can I store new fonts I've purchased or downloaded from the Internet?

Save them to */Users/username/Library/Fonts* for your personal use, or to */Library/Fonts* to allow everyone on the system access to them.

Why aren't my bitmap fonts working?

Mac OS X doesn't support bitmapped fonts—only True-Type, OpenType, and PostScript Level 1 fonts are supported by Mac OS X.

How can I make my Mac OS X fonts available in Classic Applications?

Open two Finder windows. In Window #1, go to Mac OS 9 → System Folder → Fonts; in Window #2, go to Mac OS X → Library → Fonts. In Window #2, select all the Fonts (⌘-A), then Option-drag the Mac OS X fonts into the Mac OS 9 Fonts folder in Window #1.

What does the .dfont extension mean on some of my Mac OS X fonts?

The extension stands for "Data Fork TrueType Font." Basically, this just tells you that this is a TrueType font.

How can I turn off font antialiasing?

You can't, but you can adjust the minimum font size to be affected by font smoothing in System Preferences → General → "Turn off text smoothing for font sizes *x* and smaller" (8 points is the default setting).

How do I create a Font Collection?

In TextEdit, go to Format → Font → Font Panel (⌘-T), and select Edit Collection from the pull-down menu at the bottom of the window. The title on the window will change to "Font - Collections." Click on the plus sign (+) at the lower left to add a new item in the Collections column; double-click on the name (New-1), and enter a different name (such as BookFonts), and hit Return. Select a font in the All Families column, and then click on the <<

button to add that typeface to your Family column. When you've added all the fonts, click on the Done button.

Where are my Font Collections stored, in case I want to share them with another user?

/Users/username/Library/FontCollections. If you want to share a collection, place a copy of the collection in the Shared folder. All font collections have a *.fcache* file extension.

Searching for and Locating Files

The following will help you search for and locate files:

Find a file when I don't know its name?

Finder → enter a keyword in the Search field in the toolbar → hit Return to start the search.

Finder → File → Find (⌘-F).

Index my hard drive to allow for content-based searching?

Finder → Computer → Macintosh HD → File → Get Info; click on the disclosure triangle next to "Conent index"; click on the "Index Now" button.

NOTE

The Finder does not index filenames—only the contents of files. However, you can still search for filenames.

Find a file when I can't remember where I saved it?

Use the *locate* command in the Terminal. However, you must first update the *locate* database as follows:

```
[macchuck:~] chuck% cd /usr/libexec
[macchuck:/usr/libexec] chuck% sudo ./locate.updatedb
```

If you haven't built the *locate* database yet, this command could take a few minutes to run; after which, you will be returned to the command line.

The *locate.updatedb* command is executed weekly by default, as noted in the */etc/weekly* file. However, you might want to issue this command shortly after installing Mac OS X.

Now you can use the *locate* command:

```
[macchuck:/usr/libexec] chuck% locate temp98.doc
/Users/chuck/Books/Templates/temp98.doc
[macchuck:/usr/libexec] chuck%
```

In this example, I used *locate* to search for the file *temp98.doc*; in return, the command tells me in which directory it's located.

NOTE

Indexing your hard drive via Get Info allows you to do context (keyword) searches, while building the *locate* database helps speed things up when you're searching for a filename. Use both the Finder and the command line to your advantage.

How can I speed up my Finder searches?
 Finder → Preferences → Languages for searching file contents. Click on the Select button and select the checkboxes for the languages you want to base your searches on. Unless you're working in a multilingual environment, you should select only your primary language.

Obtaining Information About the System

Use the following if you need to obtain system information:

Find out how much disk space I have left?
 Launch the Finder and look in the thin bar, just below the toolbar. You will see something that says how many items are in that directory, and how much space is available on your hard drive.

Issue the *df –k* command in the Terminal, as shown in Figure 17.

```
000              Chuck's Term — tcsh (ttyp1)
[macchuck:~] chuck% df -k
Filesystem    1K-blocks    Used    Avail Capacity  Mounted on
/dev/disk0s5  29299544 10062680 18980864    34%    /
devfs               90       90        0   100%    /dev
fdesc                1        1        0   100%    /dev
<volfs>            512      512        0   100%    /.vol
[macchuck:~] chuck%
```

Figure 17. Using df –k to display the available disk space

This shows the amount of space Used and Avail(able) for each mounted drive or partition. The / filesystem is that of Mac OS X, which on this system is at 34% capacity. Note that the numbers shown in the Used and Avail columns are listed in kilobytes, so you'll have to do some quick math to figure out the size in megabytes. (The *–m* option, which would show the size in megabytes, isn't available.)

Find out how much memory I have?
 → About This Mac.

Find out what version of Mac OS X I'm running?
 → About This Mac.

 → About This Mac; click on the version number (e.g., 10.2.1) to reveal the build number (e.g., 6D52).

Finder → Applications → Utilities → Apple System Profiler → System Profile panel. Look in the System overview section to see the exact build of Mac OS X.

Find out what version of Mac OS 9 I'm running?
In the Classic environment, use  → Apple System Profiler → System Profile panel. Look in the System overview section.

Find out what processor my Mac has?
 → About This Mac.

Finder → Applications → Utilities → Apple System Profiler → System Profile → Hardware Overview.

What type of cache do I have and how big is it?

Applications → Utilities → Apple System Profiler → System Profile → Memory Overview.

Find out whether a drive is formatted with HFS?

Applications → Utilities → Disk Utility → select the drive or partition → Information.

Find out what programs (or processes) are running?

Finder → Applications → Utilities → Process Viewer.

From the command line, using the *ps –aux* command.

From the command line, using the *top* command.

Display the status of the computer's used and free memory?

Issuing the *top* command in the Terminal will show you something similar to what's shown in Figure 18.

```
000                   Chuck's Term — tcsh (ttyp1)
Processes: 38 total, 3 running, 35 sleeping... 93 threads          21:23:40
Load Avg: 1.91, 1.96, 1.81   CPU usage: 44.2% user, 53.5% sys, 2.3% idle
SharedLibs: num =   7, resident = 2.21M code, 172K data, 580K LinkEdit
MemRegions: num = 3109, resident = 68.9M + 8.31M private, 64.8M shared
PhysMem: 65.8M wired, 60.6M active,  180M inactive,  307M used,  461M free
VM: 1.87G + 3.62M   7290(0) pageins, 0(0) pageouts

  PID COMMAND     %CPU   TIME     #TH #PRTS #MREGS RPRVT  RSHRD RSIZE  VSIZE
  391 screencapt  0.0%  0:00.05   1    22    24   128K   724K   752K  46.5M
  389 top         5.6%  0:01.59   1    14    17   204K   324K   580K  13.6M
  375 Apple Syst  0.0%  0:41.96   2    98   254  20.2M   7.53M 24.8M  92.6M
  374 Preview     0.0%  0:04.51   2    86   131  2.18M   10.2M  6.38M 81.9M
  363 ContentInd 63.1% 49:25.96   2    44   157  19.8M   3.08M 21.6M  70.8M
  354 BBEdit 6.5  0.0%  0:43.65   3    82   152  4.66M   13.8M 12.2M   133M
  351 System Pre  0.0%  0:02.79   1    80   135  3.16M   11.0M  8.17M 80.1M
  340 tcsh        0.0%  0:00.19   1    10    17   492K   652K   972K  6.00M
  339 login       0.0%  0:00.46   1    12    33   240K   376K   568K  13.7M
  338 Terminal    0.9%  0:05.55   3    65   115  1.42M   6.99M  5.84M 74.8M
  337 iChatAgent  0.0%  0:00.13   2    49    22   328K   1.24M  1.15M 15.5M
  336 InkServer   0.0%  0:03.71   1    58    92  2.17M   8.21M  4.27M 74.3M
  332 Finder     27.3% 27:19.23   2    93   152  3.79M   10.9M 12.8M  91.7M
  331 SystemUISe  0.0%  0:09.61   3   150   167  1.98M   5.50M  4.72M 72.8M
  327 Dock        0.0%  0:03.69   2    95   144  1.03M   10.4M  7.44M 73.4M
```

Figure 18. Display for the top command

The *top* command gives you a real-time view of the processes running on your system, as well as processor and memory usage. To see how much memory you have available, look at the end of the PhysMem line; in this case, I can see that my system is using 307 megabytes (307M) of RAM and that I have 461 megabytes (461M) free. To stop the *top* command from running, hit Control-C or ⌘-. to cancel the process.

View the hardware connected to my system?

Finder → Applications → Utilities → Apple System Profiler. This information can be gathered from System Profile → Hardware Overview, and from the Devices and Volumes panel.

Quickly generate a report about my system so I can submit it to Apple along with a bug report?

Launch the Terminal (*/Applications/Utilities*) and issue the following command:

```
[macchuck:~] chuck% AppleSystemProfiler > ⏎
sysprofile.txt
```

The *AppleSystemProfiler* command launches the Apple System Profiler application (*/Applications/Utilities*), and redirects the output (with the > symbol) that would normally print in the Terminal and saves it in the *sysprofile.txt* file in your home directory. Now you can open, view, and print the file using TextEdit, or copy and paste this into a bug report.

Internet, Web, and Email

Use the following settings as they relate to your Internet, web, and email usage:

Change the default email client and web browser from Mail and Internet Explorer, respectively?

To select a different email client, go to System Preferences → Internet → Email panel, and choose a different client in the Default Email Reader pull-down menu.

To select a different web browser, go to System Preferences → Internet → Web panel, and choose a different browser in the Default Web Browser pull-down menu.

Specify where files downloaded from the Internet will be saved?
System Preferences → Internet → Web panel. Click on the Select button next to "Download Files To."

Change my browser's default home page?
System Preferences → Internet → Web. Enter the new URL in the Home Page text box.

Set up a .Mac account?
System Preferences → Internet → .Mac → Sign Up. (You must be connected to the Internet to set up a .Mac account.)

Turn on web sharing?
System Preferences → Sharing → Services pane. Click on the checkbox next to Personal Web Sharing to start this service. Enabling this service allows others to access your Sites folder (*/Users/username/Sites*) from the Internet. To learn more about Personal Web Sharing, point your default browser to */Users/username/Sites/index.html*. The address for your personal web site will be: *http://yourIPAddress/~yourshortusername/*.

Register my license number for QuickTime Pro?
System Preferences → QuickTime; click on the Registration button and enter your license number.

Listen to an Internet radio station?
Dock → iTunes → Radio Tuner. Clicking on the Radio Tuner option in the Source pane to the left, the right pane will change to show you a list of different music genres from which to choose. Click on the disclosure triangle next to a music type to reveal the available stations.

Use my own stylesheet for viewing web pages in Internet Explorer?

Internet Explorer → Explorer → Preferences → Web Browser → Web Content. Select the checkbox next to "Use my style sheet," click on the Select Style Sheet button, then locate and select the Cascading Style Sheet (CSS) you want to apply.

Download a file via FTP?

If you've noticed, Mac OS X doesn't come with a graphical FTP client, such as the venerable Fetch program available (*http://www.fetchsoftworks.com*). But why bother paying for something when you can FTP files from the command line for free? For example, if you wanted to download O'Reilly's latest Word template for authors (stored in */pub/frame/templates/mswd*), you could use FTP from the Terminal as follows:

```
[macchuck:~] chuck% ftp ftp.oreilly.com
Connected to tornado.east.ora.com.
<snip>
220 tornado.east.ora.com FTP server (Version wu-2.6.
1(1)
Wed Aug 23 10:57:53 EDT 2000) ready.
Name (ftp.oreilly.com:chuck): anonymous
331 Anonymous login ok, send your complete email
address as password.
Password: username@domain.com
230 Anonymous access granted, restrictions apply.
Remote system type is UNIX.
Using binary mode to transfer files.
ftp> cd pub/frame/templates/mswd
250 CWD command successful.
ftp> ls
200 PORT command successful.
150 Opening ASCII mode data connection for /bin/ls.
total 1488
-rw-r--r--  1 61    81708 Jan 24  2001 temp.qreflet.rtf
-rw-r--r--  1 61    53775 Sep  1  2000 temp.rtf
-rw-r--r--  1 61   206848 Jan 24  2001 temp98.doc
-rw-r--r--  1 61    56801 Sep  1  2000 temp_med.rtf
-rw-r--r--  1 61    80714 Sep  1  2000 temp_prk.rtf
-rw-r--r--  1 61   196608 Sep  1  2000 temp_proc.doc
```

```
-rw-r--r--  1 61   60551 Sep  1 2000 temp_song.rtf
226 Transfer complete.
ftp> bin
200 Type set to I.
ftp> get temp98.doc
local: temp98.doc remote: temp98.doc
200 PORT command successful.
150 Opening BINARY mode data connection for temp98.doc
(206848 bytes).
226 Transfer complete.
206848 bytes received in 27.5 seconds (7514 bytes/s)
ftp> bye
221 Goodbye.
[macchuck:~] chuck%
```

The Word template (*temp98.doc*) will be saved in your
home directory, as noted by the path ([macchuck:~]). To
learn more about using FTP from the command line, see
Learning Unix for Mac OS X (O'Reilly).

Another option is to use *curl* as follows:

```
[macchuck:~] chuck% curl -O ftp://ftp.oreilly.com/pub/
frame/templates/mswd/temp98.doc
```

As you can see, the *curl* command requires the entire
path to the file you want to download; the –O option
tells *curl* to save the file to a local disk. To learn more
about *curl*, see its manpage.

*Create shortcuts on my desktop for web sites I visit often, or
for people I email frequently?*

Open the TextEdit application, and enter a URL (such as
http://www.oreilly.com) or an email address (such as
chuckdude@mac.com), then triple-click on the address to
select the entire line and drag that to your desktop. This
creates an icon on your desktop for whatever you drag
there. When you double-click on the icon, your default
web browser opens that URL, or your email client creates a new message window with the address specified by
the shortcut.

You can take this a step further by adding these shortcuts to your Favorites folder (open the Finder and click
on the Favorites heart icon in the toolbar, or press ⌘-T).

Find out how much space I have available on my iDisk?
    System Preferences → Internet → iDisk.

*Require a password from others before they can access my
iDisk's Public folder?*
    System Preferences → Internet → iDisk. Click on the
    checkbox next to "Use a Password to Protect your Pub-
    lic Folder," and then click on the Password button to set
    a password.

Modems and Dial-Up Networking

Use the following options to configure your modem and dial-
up networking:

Configure a modem for dialing into my ISP?
    Go to System Preferences → Network, and follow these
    steps:

    1. Select New Location from the Location pull-down
       menu. Enter a name for the new location (for exam-
       ple, My ISP), and click OK.
    2. Select Internal Modem from the Show pull-down
       menu.
    3. In the TCP/IP panel, select Using PPP from the Con-
       figure pull-down menu.
    4. Fill in the blanks on the PPP panel.
    5. Select your modem type from the Modem panel.
    6. Click the Apply Now button.

Show the modem status in the menu bar
    System Preferences → Network → select Internal Modem
    from the Show pull-down menu → Modem pane; click on
    the checkbox next to "Show modem status in menu bar."

Make sure my modem is working?
    Applications → Utilities → Internet Connect.

Set my computer to wake up from sleep mode when the modem rings?

System Preferences → Energy Saver → Options → Wake Options; click on the checkbox next to "Wake when the modem detects a ring."

Find out the speed of my dial-up connection?

Applications → Utilities → Internet Connect. The bottom section of the window will tell you the speed of your connection.

Disable call-waiting on my phone when using the modem?

System Preferences → Network → PPP. Insert *70 to the beginning of the telephone number you're dialing (e.g., *70, 1-707-555-1212).

Where are my modem configuration files stored?

/Library/Modem Scripts

Specify how many times my modem will redial if it detects a busy signal?

System Preferences → Network → Show → Internal Modem → PPP panel → PPP Options → Session Options.

Networking

The following settings aid with networking options:

Find the media access control (MAC) address for my Ethernet card?

Finder → Applications → Utilities → Apple System Profiler → System Profile → Network Overview → Built-in → Ethernet address.

System Preferences → Network → TCP/IP panel; toward the bottom of the window, look for a sequence of numbers and letters next to Ethernet Address.

Configure my system to connect to an Ethernet network?

Go to System Preferences → Network, and follow these steps:

1. Select New Location from the Location pull-down menu. Enter a name for the new location (for example, ORA-Local), and click OK.

2. Select Built-in Ethernet from the Show pull-down menu.

3. From the Configure pull-down menu in the TCP/IP panel, select Using DHCP if your IP address will be assigned dynamically, or Manually if your machine will have a fixed IP address. (In most cases, particularly if you have a broadband Internet connection at home, your IP address will be assigned via DHCP.)

4. If you're on an AppleTalk network, select the Make AppleTalk Active option in the AppleTalk panel, and select your Zone (if any).

5. Click the Apply Now button.

Configure my system to connect to a virtual private network (VPN)?

Here's how to set up your Mac OS X system for connecting to a VPN:

1. Launch Internet Connect (*/Applications*). (If you haven't used Internet Connect before, you will be prompted to configure the modem settings, or a VPN connection, if a modem can't be found.)

2. In the VPN Connection window, enter the Server Address, User name, and Password that you will use to connect to the VPN. If your VPN is on a Windows-based server, you will have to enter the domain as well; for example, *domain\chuck*.

3. Click the Connect button to try connecting to the VPN.

4. Open the Network preferences panel (System Preferences → Network) and select Location → New Location; supply a name for your VPN (such as "Work VPN") and hit OK.

5. Select Show → PPTP in the Network preferences panel.

6. In the TCP/IP tab, select Configure → Manually from the drop-down menu, and enter the IP address for your VPN server and the IP addresses for any DNS servers and domains to search, if needed.

7. Click the Apply Now button on the Network preferences panel.

8. Go back to Internet Connect by clicking on its Dock icon and select File → New VPN Connection Window (Shift-Command-P).

9. Click on the Connect button to connect to your VPN server. (The Status indicator in this window will tell you if you're connected or not.)

When you want to connect to the VPN in the future, follow these steps:

1. Apple → Location → _VPN Name_ (e.g., Work VPN).

2. Launch Internet Connect (*/Applications*); if you will be using the VPN frequently, you should consider adding Internet Connect to your Dock.

3. File → New VPN Connection Window (Shift-Command-P).

4. Click on the Connect button.

When you've completed the work you need to do over the VPN, click the Disconnect button in the VPN Connection window, quit Internet Connect, and then change your network location to your regular network setting.

Change my Rendezvous name from my full name to something else?

System Preferences → Sharing; enter the new name in the Rendezvous Name text box. Your Rendezvous name will have a *.local* extension; for example, *MacChuck.local*.

Configure my AirPort settings for wireless networking?

Follow the steps for connecting to an Ethernet network first, then use the AirPort Setup Assistant (*/Applications/Utilities*). The settings you've applied for your regular network will be applied to your AirPort settings.

Find out the speed of my network connection?

Network Utility (*/Applications/Utilities*) → Info panel; look next to Link Speed in the Interface Information section.

Find out what's taking a site so long to respond?

Applications → Utilities → Network Utility → Ping panel; enter the network address for the location (e.g., *www.macdevcenter.com* or *10.0.2.1*).

Use the *ping* command:

```
[macchuck:~] chuck% ping hostname
```

Trace the route taken to connect to a web page?

Network Utility (*/Applications/Utilities*) → Traceroute panel; enter the URL for the location.

Use the *traceroute* command:

```
[macchuck:~] chuck% traceroute hostname
```

Restrict access to my computer so others can get files I make available to them?

System Preferences → Sharing → File & Web panel. Click on the Start button in the File Sharing section to give others access to your Public folder (*/Users/username/Public*). The Public folder is read-only, which means that other people can only view or copy files from that directory; they cannot write files to it.

Where can my coworkers place files on my computer without getting access to the rest of my system?

With file sharing turned on, people can place files, folders, or even applications in your Drop Box, located within the Public folder (*/Users/username/Public/Drop Box*).

Quickly switch to an AirPort network after disconnecting the Ethernet cable from my iBook?

System Preferences → Network → Show → Active Network Ports. Click on the checkboxes next to the network ports you want to enable, and drag the ports in the list to place them in the order in which you're most likely to connect to them. (The Automatic location should do this for you, but it doesn't always work.)

Share my modem or Ethernet connection with other AirPort-equipped Macs?

System Preferences → Sharing → Internet panel; click on the Start button to turn Internet sharing on.

View what's inside someone else's iDisk Public folder?

Go → Connect to Server. At the bottom of the dialog box, type *http://idisk.mac.com/membername/Public*. Click Connect, or press Return; the Public iDisk image will mount on your desktop.

NOTE

Not all iDisk Public folders are created equal. An iDisk owner can choose to make her Public folder read-only, or read-write, which allows others to place files in her Public folder. The Public folder can also be password protected, which means you would need to enter a password before you can mount the Public folder.

Connect to a networked drive?

Go → Connect to Server (⌘-K).

If the server to which you want to connect is part of your local area network (LAN), click on the Local icon in the left pane, and select the server name to the right. If the server you want to connect to is part of your local Apple-Talk network, click on the AppleTalk Network icon in the left pane and select the server or computer name to the right.

Connect to an SMB share?

If you need to connect to a Windows server, you will need to specify the address in the text box as follows:

```
smb://hostname/sharename
```

After clicking the Connect button, you will be asked to supply the domain to which you wish to connect and your username and password.

NOTE

If you make a mistake, don't expect the error message to give you any assistance in figuring out why you weren't able to connect to the share.

You can speed up this process by supplying the domain and your username, as follows:

```
smb://domain;username@hostname/sharename
```

where *domain* is the NT domain name; *username* is the name you use to connect to that domain; and *hostname* and *sharename* are the server name and shared directory that you have or want access to. Now when you click on the Connect button, all you need to enter is your password (if one is required), and the networked drive will appear on your desktop.

TIP

Before pressing the Connect button, press the Add to Favorites button. This will save you time in the future if you frequently need to connect to the same drive, because you won't have to enter that address again.

Printer Configuration and Printing

Use the following options for printer configuration and printing:

Configure a printer?

Launch Print Center (*/Applications/Utilities*), and either click on the Add button in the Printer List window, or select Printer → Add Printer from the menu bar. Select how the printer is connected using the pull-down menu (AppleTalk, Directory Services, IP Printing, or USB):

- If you selected AppleTalk, select the zone (if any) using the second pull-down menu, choose the printer in the lower pane, then click the Add button.

- If you selected Directory Services, you can choose from printing via Rendezvous or to a printer listed in the NetInfo Network. Select the printer name, and then click the Add button.

- If you selected IP Printing, you will need to know and fill in the IP address of the printer; select the printer model, and click the Add button.

- If you selected USB, choose the name of the printer and the printer model, then click the Add button.

View the jobs in the print queue?

Launch the Print Center → double-click on the name of the printer to see the print queue

Cancel a print job?

Launch the Print Center → double-click on the printer name → click on the name of the print job → click on the Delete button

Halt a print job?

Launch the Print Center → double-click on the printer name → click on the name of the print job → click on the Hold button. (Click on the Resume button to start the job where it left off.)

Share the printer that's connected to my Mac with another user?

System Preferences → Sharing → Services; click on the checkbox next to Printer Sharing.

Configure my system so I can print from the command line using the Terminal?

To do this, you must first issue the cryptic *at_cho_prn* command with either the *sudo* command or as *root*:

```
[dhcp-123-45:~] chuck% sudo at_cho_prn
Password: ********
1  East_Ora_EtherTalk        2  West_Ora_EtherTalk

ZONE number (0 for current zone)? 1
Zone:East_Ora_EtherTalk
  1: 0002.83.9dtpenguin1:LaserWriter
  2: 0002.86.9d DODO1:LaserWriter
  3: 0002.82.9d Chicken1:LaserWriter
  4: 0002.08.9d Rheas1:LaserWriter
  5: 0002.85.9d weka1:LaserWriter

ITEM number (0 to make no selection)? 5
Default printer is:weka1:LaserWriter@East_Ora_
EtherTalk
status: idle
[dhcp-123-45:~] chuck%
```

In the example shown here, I've specified *East_Ora_ EtherTalk* as my AppleTalk zone and *weka1* as my default printer for printing from the command line.

View a list of available AppleTalk printers on my network?

From the command line, use the *atlookup* command:

```
[dhcp-123-45:~] chuck% atlookup
Found 156 entries in zone East_Ora_EtherTalk
0002.82.08      Chicken1:SNMP Agent
0002.82.9e      Chicken1:HP LaserJet
0002.82.9c      Chicken1:HP Zoner Responder
0002.82.9d      Chicken1:LaserWriter
0002.86.9d      DODO1:LaserWriter
0002.86.08      DODO1:SNMP Agent
```

```
0002.86.9e        DOD01:HP LaserJet
0002.86.9a        DOD01:HP Zoner Responder
0002.06.08        Kiwi:SNMP Agent
0002.06.9e        Kiwi:HP LaserJet
0002.06.9c        Kiwi:HP Zoner Responder
0002.06.9d        Kiwi:LaserWriter
0003.84.80        MacChuck:Darwin
0002.85.08        weka1:SNMP Agent
0002.85.9d        weka1:LaserWriter
0002.85.9e        weka1:HP LaserJet
0002.85.9c        weka1:HP Zoner Responder
<snip>
```

WARNING

If you're on a large AppleTalk network, *atlookup* will show you *everything*: printers, servers, computers… *everything*. You will have to look through the output to find the item you're looking for.

Send a text file to a PostScript printer?

For this, use the *enscript* and *atprint* commands:

```
[dhcp-123-45:~/Desktop] chuck% enscript -p- ↵
textFile.txt | atprint
Looking for weka1:LaserWriter@East_Ora_EtherTalk.
Trying to connect to weka1:LaserWriter@East_Ora_
EtherTalk.
atprint: printing on weka1:LaserWriter@East_Ora_
EtherTalk.
[ 3 pages * 1 copy ] left in -
[dhcp-123-45:~/Desktop] chuck%
```

The *enscript* command is used to translate plain text into PostScript so the file can be printed. The *atprint* command lets you stream any Unix output to an AppleTalk printer. In this example, the commands are piped together (using the standard Unix pipe, |), which formats the file and sends it to the default AppleTalk printer. Additional information about *enscript* and its options can be found in its manpage (*man enscript*).

NOTE

There is another Unix facility, *lpd*, for printing from the command line. However, configuring *lpd* is beyond the scope of this book. For information on how to configure *lpd* and use its associated commands (*lpr*, *lpq*, *lprm*), see *Learning Unix for Mac OS X* (O'Reilly).

Maintenance and Troubleshooting

The following settings deal with maintenance and trouble-shooting issues:

Force quit an application that's stuck?

Option-⌘-Escape opens a window showing all the running applications. Select the troublesome application and click the Force Quit button.

Option-click the application's icon in the Dock. A pop-up window will appear next to the icon with the Force Quit option; move the mouse over and release on that option.

Applications → Utilities → Process Viewer → Select the process that's causing the problem → Processes → Quit Process.

Restart my system when it's completely frozen?

Hold down the Shift-Option-⌘ keys and press the Power-On button.

Turn on crash reporting so I can see why an application crashed?

Applications → Utilities → Console → Preferences → Crashes panel; select both options. Now when an application crashes, the Console app will automatically launch and display the cause of the crash.

Where are crash logs kept?

If you've enabled crash logging, they will be stored in the *~/Library/Logs* directory.

Fix a disk that won't mount?

Applications → Utilities → Disk Utility → Select the disk that won't mount → First Aid.

My system completely froze after launching an application, what can I do?

Follow these steps:

1. Do a hard restart of your system: Control-⌘-Power-on (or Eject).

2. Log back into your system.

3. Launch the Terminal (*/Applications/Utilities*).

4. Enter the following command and hit Return:

   ```
   [macchuck:~] chuck% sudo shutdown now
   ```

   This forces an automatic shutdown of your system and takes you into single-user mode. Your screen will go black and you'll be faced with a text prompt.

5. At the prompt, enter the following command:

   ```
   sh-2.05a# fsck -y
   ```

   The *fsck* command performs a filesystem check and reports back its findings:

   ```
   bootstrap_look_up() failed (ip/send) invalid
   destination port
   bootstrap_look_up() failed (ip/send) invalid
   destination port
   bootstrap_look_up() failed (ip/send) invalid
   destination port
   ** /dev/rdisk0s2
   ** Root file system
   ** Checking HFS Plus volume.
   ** Checking Extents Overflow file.
   ** Checking Catalog file.
   ** Checking multi-linked files.
   ** Checking Catalog hierarchy.
   ** Checking volume bitmap.
   ** Checking volume information.
   ** The volume MacChuck appears to be OK.
   sh-2.05a#
   ```

6. If *fsck –y* reports that the disk has been modified, you will need to run the command again until the filesystem checks out to be OK.

7. If everything is fine, enter *reboot* at the command prompt and hit Return to reboot your system.

Partition a new hard drive?

Applications → Utilities → Disk Utility → select the new drive → Partition

Erase a CD-RW disc or hard drive?

Applications → Utilities → Disk Utility → select the CD or disk → Erase

Create a redundant array of independent disks (RAID) for my system?

Applications → Utilities → Disk Utility → Select the drives → RAID.

Access command-line mode and bypass Aqua?

There are three ways you can access the command-line interface:

1. Hold down ⌘-S when starting up the system; this is known as single-user mode.

2. At the login window, type *>console* as the username, don't enter a password, and click on the Login button. This is known as multiuser mode and is just like being in the Terminal, except that your entire screen is the Terminal.

3. From the Terminal, type *sudo shutdown now* and hit Return; this also places you in single-user mode.

When you've finished diagnosing your system, type *reboot* and press Return to reboot your system into Aqua.

Rebuild Classic's desktop?

System Preferences → Classic → Advanced panel. There is no need to rebuild Mac OS X's desktop, so holding down Option-⌘ keys at startup is futile.

All the icons on my system look funny. Is there an easy way to fix this problem?

Even though Mac OS X is more reliable than earlier versions of the Mac OS, icons and such can still go haywire. The quick fix for this problem is to delete the three "LS" files (*LSApplications*, *LSClaimedTypes*, and *LSSchemes*) in *~/Library/Preferences*.

There is a question mark icon in the Dock. What is this?

A question mark icon in the Dock or in one of the toolbars means that the application, folder, or file that the original icon related to has been deleted from your system. Just drag the question mark icon away from the Dock or toolbar to make it disappear.

I have a dual-processor G4 machine. Can I see how efficiently the processors are distributing the workload?

Applications → Utilities → CPU Monitor. Each processor will have its own meter bar.

View a log of software updates?

System Preferences → Software Update → Show Log.

How do I connect an external monitor or projector to my PowerBook without restarting?

Select → Sleep to put your laptop to sleep, plug in and turn on the display, and then hit the Escape key to wake your system and the display. You can then use the Display System Preference (System Preferences → Display) to turn display mirroring on or off as needed.

Special Characters

Included with Mac OS X is the Key Caps application (located in */Applications/Utilities*), which is a keyboard widget that allows you to see which character would be created by applying the Shift, Option, or Shift-Option keys to any key on the keyboard. Key Caps also allows you to copy and paste the character you create into another application, such as Microsoft Word.

While this might seem useful, it can be a hassle to launch another app just to create one character and copy and paste it into another program. Fortunately, one of the most little-known/-used features of the Mac OS is its ability to give you the same functionality within any application—making Key Caps unnecessary if you know what you're doing. Table 21 lists these special characters. Keep in mind that this doesn't work for all font types, and some fonts such as Symbol, Wingdings, and Zapf Dingbats create an entirely different set of characters or symbols. For example, to create the symbol for the Command key (⌘), you would need to switch the font to Wingdings and type a lowercase *z*.

Table 21. Special characters and their key mappings

Normal	Shift	Option	Shift-Option
1	!	¡	⁄
2	@	™	€
3	#	£	‹
4	$	¢	›
5	%	∞	fi
6	^	§	fl
7	&	¶	‡
8	*	•	°
9	(	ª	·
0	)	º	‚
`	~	Grave (`)[a]	’
- (hyphen)	_ (underscore)	– (en-dash)	— (em-dash)
=	+	≠	±
[	{	"	"
]	}	'	'

Table 21. Special characters and their key mappings (continued)

Normal	Shift	Option	Shift-Option
\	|	«	»
;	:	…	Ú
'	"	æ	Æ
,	<	≤	¯
.	>	≥	˘
/	?	÷	¿
a	A	å	Å
b	B	∫	ı
c	C	ç	Ç
d	D	∂	Î
e	E	Acute (´)[a]	´
f	F	ƒ	Ï
g	G	©	˝
h	H	˙	Ó
i	I	Circumflex (ˆ)[a]	ˆ
j	J	Δ	Ô
k	K	°	
l	L	¬	Ò
m	M	µ	Â
n	N	Tilde (˜)[a]	˜
o	O	ø	Ø
p	P	π	Π
q	Q	œ	Œ
r	R	®	‰
s	S	ß	Í
t	T	†	ˇ
u	U	Umlaut (¨)[a]	¨
v	V	√	◊
w	W	Σ	„

Table 21. Special characters and their key mappings (continued)

Normal	Shift	Option	Shift-Option
x	X	≈	ˋ
y	Y	¥	Á
z	Z	Ω	ˎ

^a To apply this accent, you must press another key after invoking the Option-*key* command. See Table 22.

One thing you might have noticed in Table 21 is that when the Option key is used with certain letters, it doesn't necessarily create a special character right away—you need to press another character key to apply the accent. Unlike the other Option-key commands, when used with the ˋ (backtick), E, I, N, and U characters, you can create accented characters as shown in Table 22.

Table 22. Option-key commands for creating accented characters

Key	Option-ˋ	Option-E	Option-I	Option-N	Option-U
a	à	á	â	ã	ä
Shift-A	À	Á	Â	Ã	Ä
e	è	é	ê	˜e	ë
Shift-E	È	É	Ê	˜E	Ë
i	ì	í	î	¨i	ï
Shift-I	Ì	Í	Î	ˉI	Ï
o	ò	ó	ô	õ	ö
Shift-O	Ò	Ó	Ô	Õ	Ö
u	ù	ú	û	˜u	ü
Shift-U	Ù	Ú	Û	˜U	Ü

For example, to create the acute-accented e's in the word *résumé*, you would type Option-E, and then press the E key. If you want an uppercase acute-accented E (É), press Option-E then Shift-E. Try this out with various characters in different fonts to see what sort of characters you can create.

Index

We'd like to hear your suggestions for improving our indexes. Send email to
index@oreilly.com.

Office X for Macintosh: The Missing Manual

By Nan Barber, Tonya Engst &
David Reynolds
1st Edition July 2002
728 pages, ISBN 0-596-00332-3

This book applies the urbane and
readable Missing Manuals touch to a
winning topic: Microsoft Office X
for Apple's stunning new operating
system, Mac OS X. In typical Missing Manual style, targeted sidebars
ensure that the book's three sections
impart business-level details on
Word, Excel, and the Palm-syncable
Entourage, without leaving begin-
ners behind. Indispensable reference
for a growing user base.

Macintosh Developers

Learning Cocoa with Objective-C, 2nd Edition

By James Duncan Davidson &
Apple Computer, Inc.
2nd Edition September 2002
384 pages, ISBN 0-596-00301-3

Based on the Jaguar release of Mac
OS X 10.2, this new edition of *Lear*
ing Cocoa covers the latest updates
the Cocoa frameworks, including
examples that use the Address Boo
and Universal Access APIs. Also
included with this edition is a han
quick reference card, charting
Cocoa's Foundation and AppKit
frameworks, along with an Appenc
that includes a listing of resources
essential to any Cocoa developer—
beginning or advanced. This is the
"must-have" book for people who
want to develop applications for M
OS X, and is the only book approv
and reviewed by Apple engineers.

Learning Carbon

By Apple Computer, Inc.
1st Edition May 2001
368 pages, ISBN 0-596-00161-4

Get up to speed quickly on creatir
Mac OS X applications with Carbc
You'll learn the fundamentals and
key concepts of Carbon programming as you design and build a cc
plete application under the book's
guidance. Written by insiders at
Apple Computer, *Learning Carbon*
provides information you can't get
anywhere else, giving you a head
start in the Mac OS X application
development market.

O'REILLY®

ac OS X Hacks

Rael Dornfest
Kevin Hemenway
Edition March 2003
0 pages, ISBN 0-596-00460-5

ac OS X Hacks reflects the real-
orld know how and experience of
ose well steeped in Unix history
d expertise, sharing their no-non-
nse, sometimes quick-and-dirty
lutions to administering and tak-
g full advantage of everything a
nix desktop has to offer: Web,
ail, and FTP serving, security ser-
ces, SSH, Perl and shell scripting,
mpiling, configuring, scheduling,
tworking, and hacking.

coa in a Nutshell

Mike Beam
t Edition May 2003
0 pages, ISBN 0-596-00462-1

side from material that Apple
cludes with its Developer Tools,
ry little documentation exists to
ver Cocoa's Objective-C Frame-
orks—vital tools for anyone inter-
ted in developing applications for
ac OS X. This new title provides a
mplete overview of Cocoa's object
asses with a series of chapters in
e first half of the book, and a
uick reference to Cocoa's Founda-
on and Application Kit (AppKit)
asses in the second half.

Cocoa Design Patterns

By Erik M. Buck
1st Edition August 2003 (est.)
384 pages (est.), ISBN 0-596-00430-3

As more users "switch" from Unix
and Windows to the Mac, program-
mers need to stay ahead of the curve
and develop their applications using
Apple's Cocoa frameworks. This
book illustrates the core design patterns of Cocoa programming, and
transfers knowledge about the struc-
ture and rationale of Cocoa; something that isn't covered in any other
book in print. The book explains the
essential patterns of objects that are
used in Cocoa, and describes problems solved by Cocoa and the conse-
quences of each solution.

O'REILLY®

To order: 800-998-9938 • order@oreilly.com • www.oreilly.com
Online editions of most O'Reilly titles are available by subscription at safari.oreilly.com
Also available at most retail and online bookstores.